A Short Guide to Writing
about Music

THE SHORT GUIDE SERIES

Under the Editorship of
Sylvan Barnet and Marcia Stubbs

A Short Guide to Writing about Music

JONATHAN BELLMAN
University of Northern Colorado

LONGMAN

An imprint of Addison Wesley Longman, Inc.

New York • Reading, Massachusetts • Menlo Park, California • Harlow, England
Don Mills, Ontario • Sydney • Mexico City • Madrid • Amsterdam

Sponsoring Editor: Lynn M. Huddon
Marketing Manager: Renée Ortbals
Project Manager: Bob Ginsberg
Design Manager: Rubina Yeh
Cover Illustration: Pablo Picasso, "Guitar and Wine Glass," 1912 (collage and charcoal). Collection of the McNay Art Museum, bequest of Marion Koogler McNay. © 1999 Estate of Pablo Picasso/Artists Rights Society (ARS), New York.
Electronic Production Specialist: Heather A. Peres
Senior Print Buyer: Hugh Crawford
Electronic Page Makeup: Allentown Digital Services Division of RR Donnelley & Sons Company
Printer and Binder: RR Donnelley & Sons Company
Cover Printer: Coral Graphic Services, Inc.

Library of Congress Cataloging-in-Publication Data

Bellman, Jonathan, (date)-
    A short guide to writing about music / Jonathan Bellman.
      p.   cm.—(The short guide series)
    Includes index.
    ISBN 0-321-01577-0
    1. Music—Historiography Handbooks, manuals, etc. 2. Musical criticism—Authorship Handbooks, manuals, etc. I. Title.
ML3797.B4   1999
808'.06678—dc21   99-14759
                                            CIP

Please visit our website at http://www.awlonline.com

ISBN 0-321-01577-0

345678910—DOC—020100

For my parents:

Samuel Irving Bellman
(Professor Emeritus of English, California State Polytechnic University, Pomona), who devoted much of his professional life to teaching writing to the undergraduates of the state of California

Jeanne Lisker Bellman
who taught her sons

Contents

Preface

People who devote their lives to music are a passionate and quixotic lot, from primary school music teacher to international concert artist, from local concert reviewer to professional scholar and researcher. Writing about music demands the same wild-eyed commitment that we give to teaching, playing, and studying it, as well as the same dogged practice to ensure that the end product reflects balance and control—*not* quixotic, wild-eyed commitment. I seek to provide some guidance both for freeing and controlling the inner writer.

After an introductory chapter, *A Short Guide to Writing about Music* is largely organized by task, such as writing reviews, analyses, essays, research papers, and preparing a final manuscript. Because the different genres of writing about music have different requirements and protocols, this seemed to be the most pragmatic way of going about it; readers would know exactly where to go. With this in mind, Chapter 1 (and perhaps Chapter 2, depending on the reader's background) should probably be read first, and the following chapters should be read in an order reflecting the reader's needs or curricular demands. But there is a good deal of cross-applicability: Chapter 8, "Style in Writing," is relevant to all writers, as are the instructions regarding musical examples in Chapter 9, the section "Hints on Beginning" in Chapter 5, and so on. Probably the best way to begin to use this book is to skim it in its entirety, so as to gain a sense of what may be found in it and where it may be found.

This book does not seek to duplicate or supersede a work such as *The Elements of Style* by William Strunk, Jr., and E. B. White; that prodigiously concise book ought to be required reading for every English-language writer of any discipline. Similarly, the style manual by Kate L. Turabian (*A Manual for Writers of Term Papers, Theses, and Dissertations*, 6th ed. [Chicago and London: University of Chicago Press, 1996]) goes into far more detail regarding guidelines than I am able to do here.

ACKNOWLEDGMENTS

Those who have contributed to my knowledge of writing are many, and I can hope to acknowledge only a very few here. My dear friend and former doctoral advisor George Barth of Stanford University read and marked draft after draft of my papers and dissertation, patiently offering suggestions; much of what I have subsequently achieved is due to his generosity and dedication. Ralph P. Locke of the Eastman School of Music and Mark DeVoto of Tufts University gave helpful advice and generously shared documents they had prepared on writing about music. John Michael Cooper of the University of North Texas and Marian Wilson Kimber of Cornell College of Iowa gave me valuable input on teaching research skills. The late Steven Gilbert of California State University, Fresno, read a draft of Chapter 3 and made several excellent suggestions; I grieve that he didn't live to see the final product. I offer a deep bow of gratitude to Ed Loomis, my undergraduate writing teacher (formerly of the University of California, Santa Barbara), who set me straight on summaries and abstracts at a very early point in my writing career.

Permissions for quoted material were graciously provided by Oxford University Press, Musica Rara Publications, and *Stereo Review/High Fidelity*. European American Music Distributors Corporation, agents for Schott Musik International, were very helpful in providing permissions for the use of the Ligeti score excerpts in Tim Sullivan's research paper in Chapter 7.

My chief editor at Addison Wesley Longman, Sylvan Barnet, has been a model: prompt in his reading, thorough and clear in his annotation, and constructive in his criticism. The editorial team (Patricia Rossi, Lynne Cattaffi, and Lynn Huddon) has been unfailingly helpful and encouraging, and has made the production of this book a far pleasanter experience than it otherwise might have been. This book was also blessed with a fine, committed group of readers for the submitted manuscript: James M. Anthony, Towson University; Mauro Botelho, Davidson College; Michael J. Budds, University of Missouri-Columbia; John Michael Cooper, University of North Texas; John J. Deal, Florida State University; Michael Farley, St. Lawrence University; Marian Wilson Kimber, Cornell College; Steven Plank, Oberlin College; and Gordon Thompson, Skidmore College. They reviewed the draft in painstaking detail, offered insightful suggestions, and every one of them has made a substantial contribution to this book. I am deeply grateful.

I have learned at least as much from my writing students as I hope to teach by writing this book; to them, for their general patience and good humor when receiving assignment after assignment covered in red ink, I am very grateful. Those who have generously allowed me to use their work in this book have been particularly helpful: Kristin Kremers, Dawn Kummer, Matthew Larson, Amie Margoles, Jessica Mosier, and Tim Sullivan. I am grateful to Susan Nelson, the Director of Arts Information at the University of Northern Colorado, for allowing me to use two of her press releases, and also to my colleague (and beloved wife) Dr. Deborah Kauffman for the use of her concert program annotations. Both she and our son Benjamin bore the family pressures occasioned by this book with good humor and forbearance.

JONATHAN BELLMAN

A Short Guide to Writing about Music

1

Writing about Music

There is so much talk about music and so little is said. I believe that words are not at all up to it, and if I should find that they were adequate I would stop making music altogether.[1]

—FELIX MENDELSSOHN

WORDS ABOUT MUSIC: WHY?

Most musicians can sympathize with the composer Robert Schumann's famous musing, "But why so many words about music? The best discourse on music is silence. . . . Away with your musical journals!" Even acknowledging the irony of Schumann's comment—he helped found a music journal and served as its chief editor for roughly eleven years— many would agree that there seems to be something odd, almost wasteful, about the number of words written about music, an art needing no words to exist. Another nineteenth-century figure, the essayist and critic Walter Pater, apparently agreed: "All art," he wrote, "constantly aspires to the condition of music," and it is tempting to conclude that prose treatments of music are therefore superfluous. What already resides on Mt. Olympus, so to speak, has no need of wings to get there.

If, as Pater implies, the other arts seek to achieve what music already has, students may find the comments of Mendelssohn and Schumann attractive. If there is little point to writing about music, after all, then there

---

[1]Mendelssohn, letter of 15 October 1842, quoted in *Source Readings in Music History* (1950), ed. Oliver Strunk, vol. 6 (rev. edn.), *The Nineteenth Century*, ed. Ruth Solie (New York: W. W. Norton, 1998), 159.

is less point in reading about how to write about it. But (before you glee-fully shut this book) are we sure what Pater meant? Does he suggest that all art seeks to be lovely, or to produce certain emotions within the lis-tener's soul? That all art seeks to function as light entertainment, to allow us at least a vague pleasure when our full attention is not focused, or to motivate us to a particular behavior, such as dancing or sleeping? Cer-tainly, different kinds of music can do all these things. Or, rather, did Pa-ter mean that the other arts envy music's capacity for direct-to-the-heart communication, its freedom from words and representative images?

The questions raised by Pater's seemingly clear assertion illustrate the need for writing about music. They also indicate why it is such a tricky business. A constant in civilization since ancient times, music has always been notoriously hard to describe; such questions as how it "works," what effect it has on listeners, and what point it seeks to make are frequently asked but never fully answered. In a sense, then, there is never enough writing about music. Every writer has, potentially, some-thing to contribute.

Just what this contribution is may not initially be apparent. In my ex-perience as a writer and teacher, worthwhile ideas result most often from insistent questioning of and dogged reflection upon the subject. The questioning should happen before the writing begins in earnest and as the early drafts develop. I do not mean to suggest that the idea-generat-ing process stops when the writing begins; further ideas will certainly evolve throughout the writing process. In fact, a substantial school of thought promotes "free writing" as a means of finding ideas in the first place—that is, if you begin writing, ideas will follow. Ultimately, the cir-cumstances under which ideas present themselves are unique to every writer. But I firmly believe that before pen meets paper (or fingers meet keyboard), the author must have *some* idea of the points that need to be made. To put it another way, writing is the process that will ultimately fashion ideas, once they exist, into clear and coherent form. Writing in order to arrive at those ideas in the first place seems a bit premature—re-vising before there is anything to revise. But however the ideas are first produced, once they are in place, the real writing begins.

The author's primary obligation is twofold. First, ideas must be ex-pressed with a certain degree of confidence. The author must believe in them, certain that he or she is not merely parroting clichés or casually ac-quired thoughts too new or unexamined to defend. Second, the author must distrust what at the moment seem to be good ideas, and he or she must be willing to go through a painful evaluation process, revising draft after draft in an effort to refine the idea and perfect the mode of expression. Writing is both art and craft, and it requires as much work as does music-making itself—perfecting one's instrumental or vocal expertise or developing a personal compositional language. The initial draft, the first exposition of ideas, is only the beginning of an arduous process.

This may seem daunting. How can one be confident of his or her ideas and writing, yet still know when to be dissatisfied with a draft? How can one go about expressing opinions and summarizing research when the intended audience (a professor, say) has a good deal more experience and training? How can one even *begin*, given the risks?

Answer: start somewhere. Start where you are right now.

CHOOSING AN AUDIENCE

Judging from the remark quoted at the beginning of this chapter, Mendelssohn might well have agreed with an even more blunt observation: a good deal of writing on musical subjects fails utterly. This failure has less to do with the use of advanced musical vocabulary, a common complaint, than with the neglect of two key questions that must be answered before writing begins. They are: For whom am I writing? and How can I best reach this audience? These seemingly obvious questions require careful consideration. The answers will ultimately dictate the amount of technical terminology, the level of prose, the length of the analytical discussions, and the balance between musical and nonmusical material (historical background, for example) that you adopt.

For example, the opening phrase "Beethoven, German-born and reared in the Classical tradition" would probably be inappropriate for a music major's music history paper because all of this information is common knowledge to the professor and the author's classmates. On the other hand, newspaper readers or a concert audience might find this information helpful because it turns a name into a human being. Conversely, if in writing about Beethoven's piano sonata, op. 53 ("Waldstein") one comments on how interesting it is that the second theme of the first movement is introduced in the mediant rather than the dominant key, only trained musicians will have any idea what is being discussed.

Writing too ambitiously for either the reader or one's own level of experience can be even more inappropriate. For example, a sentence that begins "Since Beethoven was a titan who spanned Classical and Romantic eras" will be meaningless to virtually everyone, even though it is the sort of bromide often encountered in music appreciation texts and recording liner notes. Novice readers with no knowledge of style periods will not understand what such a sentence means, and those with more musical experience will know that this statement is by no means the truism it seems to be. Such a statement cannot be made without addressing the extent to which Beethoven was Classicist or Romantic, the ways in which he might be considered a "titan," and so on. One of the most basic rules of writing is that the author never make statements he or she is not prepared to defend.

We will return to these issues as we discuss specific types of writing. Let it suffice here to say that successful writing about music amounts to far more than the correct use of terminology. Awareness of one's audience and tailoring a writing style and content to their understanding are all-important if an author hopes to be read and understood.

KINDS OF WRITING

Only a portion of "writing about music" consists of discussion of the music itself. Other necessary components include biographical and historical background, discussions of instruments, considerations of the ways music is understood in society, and inquiries into music's relationship to the other arts and to the wider culture. An essay, paper, column, or book about music may approach the music from an analytical standpoint (examining just how musical works "work"), or it may address performance matters, cultural contexts, the physical source material for the music, or any number of other perspectives. Above all, writers must be aware of the variety of tools available.

Here are some common approaches to writing about music.

Biography and History

Biography and history are genres of writing that examine the people and circumstances that produced a work or a repertory, situating works in the musical and cultural environments of their time. This information, relevant in some measure to almost any kind of writing about music, is particularly valued among the general readership. Of biography, James Parakilas writes:

[I]t may be that many people like to read biographies of musicians because no other kind of writing about music has meaning for them. But there is also a positive attraction that draws people to the lives of musicians . . . .[2]

Parakilas goes on to identify the intimacy that people feel for their favorite performers and the fascination many have with the musical life. Biographical treatment lets readers gain additional personal, musical, or psychological insight into the composers and performers of the music they love. Its appeal is such that for many, biography is their first (and possibly only) venture beyond listening.

Historical and biographical treatments of musical subjects can overlap a good deal. History is made up of the doings of people, after all, and individuals cannot properly be studied in the absence of historical context. In an introductory note, after telling us that "this book is not a biography in the ordinary sense," the author of a famous example of such a blend comments:

In the battle of Berlioz with his age a typical story is dramatized by the events themselves. History spins the plot around the Artist, and the four corners of our society are illumined like a stage. For in a high civilization all social facts and forces become the matrix, and sometimes the subject, of the artist's work; and in the forms and conditions of a collective art like music we find again the elements of familiar history—politics, economics, and the struggles of human groups.[3]

Depending on epoch, sometimes individuals disappear into the historical fog for lack of records. A study of Florentine Renaissance carnival songs, for example, will of necessity dwell not on the composers but on the songs themselves and their carnival circumstances because substantial information on the majority of the composers is lost. But when biographical information is available, it will often be an important element of a historical study. Biographical and historical studies can be among the most easy to read and assimilate, and they speak to the entire musically inclined readership.

---

[2]James Parakilas, "Concerning Biographies . . ." *The College Music Society Newsletter* (January 1995), 6.

[3]Jacques Barzun, *Berlioz and the Romantic Century*, 2 vols. (Boston: Little, Brown, 1950), I, [xvi].

Style Study

Style studies take as their point of departure music's raw materials, its melodies, harmonies, meters and rhythms, scoring, and other basic ingredients. How these core elements become a "style" suitable for examination may be better illustrated by example than by description. Let us glance at the American children's folk song, "Go Tell Aunt Rhody" (shown in Example 1.1).

The text itself is mock-solemn, gravely acknowledging a death. Death in the adult world would occasion mourning, and indeed later verses have the gander and goslings weeping. But that this is really a children's joke is shown by the second line, "she died in the mill-pond, stand-

Go Tell Aunt Rhody

American Folk Song

EX. 1.1
American children's folk song, "Go Tell Aunt Rhody."

ing on her head."[4] The music, known to children all over the United States from folk and school settings, complements the text in several ways. That is, the musical *materials* are completely appropriate to the words and to the message they convey.

1. The melody consists of only five notes. These are the first five notes of a major scale, playable on the piano without moving one's hand, as melodies for beginners tend to be. So not only is the tune short, simple, and easy to play, its range (a fifth) easily accommodates the limited range of an untrained child's voice, making it easy to sing. The melody thus strongly suggests childlike music-making but without alluding, as Mozart and others did, to the timeless childhood taunt heard in the pitches G-G-E-A-G-E.

2. The rhythmic vocabulary is simple, suggesting childhood. There are no syncopations or rhythmic complexities. Motion is based on an even quarter-note pulse in $\frac{4}{4}$ time, phrases are short and even, and there is no rhythmic value shorter than the quarter notes.

3. The harmony is as simple as possible. There are only two chords, tonic and dominant, so the harmonic language is reduced to the chord that gives the greatest sense of rest and repose (the tonic) and the chord that most wants to go to it (the dominant). The harmony thus has a warm, familiar, and reassuring effect.

There is more, but the point is made: the musical language of this song, the composite sound produced by its materials, mirrors the text. The text bespeaks simplicity, and the music is composed of the most basic materials available. The *style* of this song, in other words, perfectly suits its message.

Style studies often proceed from a perspective of actual or implied comparison, which is necessary in order to answer a variety of questions. Conclusions may involve identification of the composer; dating of the work, as when the style of a piece is found to be more typical of a composer's earlier rather than later writing; national style or influence; or even where a composer got certain musical ideas. But the basis of style inquiry is musical materials, what a piece of music is made of, and what makes its sound distinctive.

One natural outgrowth of style study consists of investigations into what particular styles meant to their original audiences. The musical language chosen by a composer often holds meanings for its contemporary

---

[4]"Milk-pond" is another, less coherent variant.

audience that are lost to later generations of listeners. Jazz provides a good example: what is now a popular and honored American idiom originally had connotations of sexuality, decadence, even danger. These disreputable implications became particularly significant when the jazz language was used in concert works; the use of what was perceived as a low-class, forbidden music in an elevated concert context had a powerful effect on audiences of the 1920s and 1930s.[5] Today's average concertgoer, happy to hear frequent performances of popular Gershwin and Ravel works, probably has little idea of what the raw materials in such music originally meant. A style study on this topic might point out both what elements are jazz-derived ("blue notes," for example, and certain dance rhythms), and how the music was understood, thus addressing both materials and significance.

Analysis

Analysis consists of coming to an understanding of the structure and processes of a piece, or "how it works." It differs from style study in that it primarily investigates how the notes of a piece relate to each other rather than to a widely understood musical language or to extramusical ideas. Analysts proceed from a variety of approaches, including harmonic (or vertical), melodic (or linear), textural, and rhythmic. It is impossible to analyze music (or to understand another's analysis) without full musical literacy and a command of technical vocabulary. Accordingly, analyses usually make the toughest reading, not only because of the density of the subject matter, but because of the necessity for frequent reference to score examples. The best analyses are written by those with a good deal of experience with music study. Chapter 3 addresses the challenges of writing musical analysis.

Performance Study

Discussion and evaluation of the way music works in performance are central to writing on musical subjects. The concert review relies primarily on this perspective, but any musical writing gains substantially by viewing

---

[5]The first such usage was in 1923, Darius Milhaud's *La Création du monde,* although Ives, Debussy, and Stravinsky had used ragtime previous to this.

music within a performance context. All aspects of the performance situation are relevant: how well the performer(s) did, how coherent and effective a piece is as performed (as opposed to its potential on paper), how it makes the listener feel, and its overall effect. Performance studies inquire into the way music operates in real time, rather than consider music as text.

A subcategory of performance studies is *Performance Practices,* which investigates the historical context of musical performance. The underlying assumption of this discipline is that a knowledge of historical performance circumstances is necessary for a solid understanding of any music, including the most often heard masterworks. Among the elements of historical performance are: period instruments and how they sounded (as closely as we can approximate them); how much and what kinds of ornamentation needed to be supplied by the performer; techniques and methods of playing the instruments; the size and seating (or standing) arrangement of ensembles; performance etiquette for musicians and audience alike; performance spaces and the acoustics they had; and the ways in which musical notations, both archaic and current, have been understood and realized in performance.

Organological Study

Organology is the study of musical instruments both historical and modern, their mechanical aspects, physical properties, and capabilities. Because much music is written with certain instruments in mind, the character of those instruments has a profound effect on how the music is written and how it sounds. Writing about organological matters frequently involves descriptions of mechanical apparatus and physical motion, and it is thus often highly technical.

Archival Study

Archival studies are most commonly associated with music at least several centuries old, music which survives principally in manuscripts. Information of any kind about this music is fragmentary, but some facts may be gleaned from such documents as pay receipts, court and church records, baptismal certificates, and death notices, all of which survive principally in archives (hence "archival"). Much of what we know about music of the Middle Ages and Renaissance is the result of searching through manuscripts and documents. When such studies deal with large numbers of pieces and statistical information, the results are often presented in tabular form.

Source Study

A related area of study investigates musical documents themselves: multiple versions of works, compositional sketches, and variant published editions. Such studies are not limited to early music, but they share with archival studies the necessity of painstaking examination of primary sources. This examination frequently involves the decoding of smudged writing and the identifications of paper type, ink composition, and handwriting. Like archival studies, the attention to such details is always in the interest of a broader musical and historical goal, such as a better understanding of a composer's compositional process or a clear picture of the dissemination patterns of a particular repertory.

CRITICISM

Music criticism consists of the explanation and evaluation of works or performances. Like analysis, music criticism may be accomplished in a variety of ways. Common to all forms of critical writing is the assumption that it is based on informed opinion; one (presumably authoritative) author's view is intended to inform and illuminate many readers.

The idea of "informed opinion" can be confusing. Embedded in this common phrase are two discrete but overlapping concepts: *opinions* and *values*. Opinions are what we desire and expect from critics, but we have a right to expect more than "I just can't stand Wagner," "the violinist understands Bach perfectly because she used Galamian's bowings," or "concert music composed in this century is raucous and incoherent." These three simple statements of preference approach a chocolate-vs.-vanilla level of subjectivity, for which reason they may not profitably be disputed. They might seem authoritative, but they are not.

Every critic proceeds from personal values (that is, principles or standards) which ideally represent more than mere preferences, which presumably were adopted after some consideration, and which may be expected to stand up to critical scrutiny and debate. These values might include "live performance is integral to musical art," "the study of historical performance traditions and techniques leads to better understanding of the music," or "support of music by living composers keeps the concert tradition vital." Advocates of recordings-as-performance might challenge the first example, partisans of traditional conservatory education might dispute the second, and many contemporary listeners would dispute the third. (But compare these dissenting positions with, for example, "Wagner is great" or "twentieth-century music *is not* raucous and incoherent," which are still no more than opinions.) Plausible objections help establish ideas as *values*—philosophical stances—that will inform critical evaluations and support or refute other critical opinions. This emphasis on both the principles that guide critical judgment and the *reasoning* that proceeds from them makes them something very different from mere opinions.

One common type of criticism is the concert review. This staple of music journalism, generally intended for a wide readership, seeks to evaluate what took place at a particular event, both to offer an assessment for the benefit of those who were not able to attend and to provide another perspective for those who did, not only describing what was played and how well, but offering commentary reflecting the reviewer's values and beliefs. (For more discussion of the reviewing process, see Chapter 2.) A related journalistic genre, though one requiring more experience, is program and liner notes, which normally provide brief discussions of works to be performed in concert or included on a recording. Here, explanation is far more important than evaluation; the goal is to enhance the listening experience for a broad range of listeners. (For more on this kind of writing, see Chapter 4.)

More specialized music criticism often examines the music in terms of beauty, effectiveness, or artistic merit. One of the most common techniques is comparison: works of the same or similar genres, or historical periods, or composers, may be examined in light of each other. A clearer picture of a work is thus achieved by viewing it in a broader musical environment.

Still another type of criticism examines music in the light of culture and society, past and present. A critique of this kind takes as its departure point the idea that musical works do not appear in a vacuum; they reflect, in key ways, the perspectives of the society and composers that produce them. As later listeners probably have radically different perspectives and experience, such commentaries on the hearing, perception, and "meaning" of music seek to place it in a multiplicity of contexts and to examine its significance outside the concert hall and classroom. There are several common approaches to this kind of criticism.

Cultural Criticism

Criticism from the perspective of social or cultural history examines the way music relates to its cultural surroundings, whether these surroundings are from its own time or the present. Susan McClary encapsulated the concerns of cultural criticism in her study of a Mozart piano concerto movement, a work which

> neither makes up its own rules nor derives them from some abstract, absolute, transcendental source. Rather it depends heavily on conventions of eighteenth-century harmonic syntax, formal procedure, genre type, rhythmic propriety, gestural vocabulary, and associations. All of these conventions have histories: *social* histories marked with national, economic, class, and gender—that is, political—interests.[6]

Not only the work as a whole, therefore, but every aspect of it is to be considered in the light of the greater culture. So, for example, because jazz emerged from various African-American musical styles around the beginning of the twentieth century, it can be studied not only for its musical content but for the associations listeners had with the African-American musicians who played it, and what such music was thought to convey. Note how this connection between music-as-played and its societal significance dovetails with the jazz example discussed above under Style Study. This correspondence illustrates both that the boundaries separating different types of musical writing are hazy at best, and that different perspectives often inform and supplement one another.

Feminist Criticism

Music criticism from a feminist perspective proceeds from the idea that the genders of composers and listeners affect not only how music is produced and heard, but also how it is received in society. Feminist criticism is not simply criticism by women or criticism of women musicians; it has addressed a variety of new topics. As Patrice Koelsch suggests,

---

[6]Susan McClary, "A Musical Dialectic from the Enlightenment: Mozart's *Piano Concerto in G Major, K. 453,* Movement 2," *Cultural Critique* (Fall 1986): 133-34. Reprinted by permission of Oxford University Press.

one of the original methodologies of feminist criticism is to look for the gaps and listen for the silences. We must learn to see and hear what has been invisible and inaudible to us.[7]

As this field has grown, there has been great interest in rediscovering and publicizing female composers and their music, studying this music in light of the established repertory, and reexamining the established repertory with this much-less-familiar repertory in mind. In a study of the seventeenth-century Florentine singer and composer Barbara Strozzi, musicologist Ellen Rosand explains why much of the music by women from this period does not survive by identifying the differing roles and circumstances of performer and composer in the Florentine musical world, in addition to those of female and male.

> Although numerous contemporary reports and descriptions bear witness to the existence of highly skilled female singers who graced the courts and theaters of seventeenth-century Italy, we know few compositions by secular women of the period. It is difficult to believe, however, that none of the most celebrated female singers wrote music—at least for their own use. There seems no reason to assume that, in this respect, they would have differed in ability from the ubiquitous, highly esteemed, and famous male singer-composers of the early part of the century. Yet the fact remains that we have very little of their music.
>
> For singers—female as well as male—creating at least some of the music they performed may well have been such an integral aspect of their activity that it was simply taken for granted, viewed as a normal part of the performer's task. If such music has not survived, part of the reason must lie in the fact that it was neither printed nor copied in manuscripts. It may have been partly or totally improvised and thus never committed to paper, even originally. For whatever reason, it was apparently not prized as an object independent of its performance.[8]

---

[7]Patrice Koelsch, "The Criticism of Quality and the Quality of Criticism," *Art Papers* (November-December 1990), 14.

[8]Ellen Rosand, "The Voice of Barbara Strozzi," in *Women Making Music: The Western Art Tradition, 1150-1950*, ed. Jane Bowers and Judith Tick (Urbana, IL and Chicago: University of Illinois Press, 1986), 173.

Feminist criticism also seeks to address somewhat subtler previously neglected questions. Do the different genders tend to compose and perform different kinds of music? Do they hear and interpret music differently? What does music signify for their respective places in society? How does the "gendering" (i.e., associating with or characterizing by a particular gender) of a musical genre affect its subsequent reception? Many of the questions raised by this emerging discipline have sought to broaden the context for music study, reception, and understanding.

Gay and Lesbian Criticism

Gay and lesbian criticism, which has much in common with feminist criticism, is often linked with it in an area called "gender studies." Following the feminist critical model, gay criticism (sometimes called Queer Theory, with intentional confrontationalism) has taken particular care to reexamine the music of familiar composers who were gay, such as Chaikovsky and Britten, in light of their sexual preferences, perspectives, and the pressures they felt from society. Another interest of gay criticism has been the hidden significances, the encoding of nontraditional meanings in seemingly traditional music, that resulted from the long history of camouflage, denial, and concealed practices and desires. For example, recent studies have sought to identify the representations of gay sexuality in the music of Copland and Schubert.[9]

All critical approaches are personal, and by definition would make no claim to objectivity. Gay and lesbian criticism is the most unabashedly personal of all, often blending criticism with open autobiography, even sexual autobiography. The subheadings of Suzanne Cusick's essay "On a Lesbian Relationship with Music: A Serious Effort Not to Think Straight," for example, are:

Why am I talking about this?
Sexuality and Musicality: what am I talking about?

[9]David Metzer, "Phantom Voices: Homoeroticism in Works by Blitzstein and Copland," paper delivered at the 1993 meeting of the American Musicological Society in Montréal, Québec; Susan McClary, "Constructions of Subjectivity in Schubert's Music," *Queering the Pitch: The New Gay and Lesbian Musicology,* ed. Philip Brett, Elizabeth Wood, and Gary C. Thomas (New York and London: Routledge, 1994), 205-233.

"Being" a lesbian: what do I mean?

"Who's on top?"

What if music IS sex?[10]

Gender Studies thus both critiques what are perceived to be the dominant paradigms in music reception, interpretation, and understanding, and it openly celebrates music's sensuality and its relationship to other sensual experiences. It is a specialized area in music criticism, one that continually develops its own vocabulary and approaches, and about which there continues to be a good deal of debate.

Marxist Criticism

Marxist criticism, common in the Soviet Union before the fall of the Berlin Wall, is most important in musical writing for its influence. Marxist political thought posits a fundamental opposition and enmity between workers (who were considered to be politically and economically powerless) and their employers (who held power over the workers), and before them between the peasantry and the nobility. Marxism sees a historical inevitability in the demise of a capitalist power structure that is as doomed as the feudal system was before it. The following passage, about an old Hungarian folk song in which an elderly villager gives directions to his master (text: "Gaffer, gaffer, which is the way to Becskerek? Master, master, this is the way to Becskerek"), illustrates the Marxist stance.

> This simple, popular melody, or fragment of a melody, consisting of four notes . . . represents the earliest written record of Hungarian music. It is on the boundary of the old and the new period and with it begins the history of Hungarian music recorded in musical notation. It would seem that the "peasant voice" inherent in this music often "showed the way" when the culture of the rulers had a tendency to go astray, and it was a strange reminder at a time when the suppression of the peasant revolts and the petrification of the feudal society, amid the

---

[10]Suzanne Cusick, "On a Lesbian Relationship with Music: A Serious Effort Not to Think Straight," in *Queering the Pitch: The New Gay and Lesbian Musicology,* ed. Philip Brett, Elizabeth Wood, and Gary C. Thomas (New York and London: Routledge, 1994) 67-83.

increasing exactions of Vienna and Constantinople[,] bore the country
the catastrophe of Mohács, and centuries of crises.[11]

Marxist art and literary criticism have often been preoccupied with
polarities: individual vs. society, member of an excluded group vs. the
majority, have-not vs. have. Many strains of critical thought show a clear
influence of earlier Marxist thinking: certain kinds of cultural criticism
see an eternal divide between the powerful and the powerless, feminist
criticism sometimes views music from the perspective of woman as
perennially marginalized Other, and gay and lesbian criticism may see an
irreconcilable polarity between traditional, heterosexually oriented society on one hand and, on the other, the lifestyles, needs, rights, and perspectives of gays, lesbians, and transgender individuals.

THE AUTHOR'S OPINION: CLARITY AND RESTRAINT

In written criticism in particular, and in all writing about music to some
extent, there can be no pretense of airtight "proof" or scientific accuracy.
The author's opinion can never be fully suppressed, no matter how stren-
uous his or her efforts at "objectivity" may be. This is all to the good; writing is done by human beings, and human beings have values and opinions,
register emotional responses, and come to personal conclusions. Decisions regarding which aspects of a musical passage are most salient, what
issues should be addressed, and how one should approach a subject all
testify to a particular posture and opinion on the part of the author. Complete objectivity is a fiction and should not be pursued as an ideal.

On the other hand, convincing writing on music (or on any subject,
for that matter) does not take frequent recourse to unfounded assertions
prefaced by "I feel," "it seems to me," "to my mind," and the like. Although these phrases are inherently unobjectionable, you should use

---

[11]Bence Szabolcsi, *A Concise History of Hungarian Music*, trans. Sára Karig
(London: Barrie & Rockliff in cooperation with Corvina Press in Budapest,
1964), 23. Szabolcsi was for a long time one of the central figures in Hungarian
musicology, and particularly because of the publication date I suspect that the inclusion of this passage had more to do with the Soviet censors than with his own
historical view.

them with discretion. Readers have a right to believe that what they are reading is based on more than the author's opinion, even when it is clearly an opinion piece. Those authors who ground their opinions in solid evidence and reasoning—or at least in clearly formulated values— are persuasive, while those who merely vent unfounded opinions (in essence, running off at the pen) are wasting the reader's time.

Consider the opening of the second movement of Mozart's piano concerto in A major, K. 488 (shown in Example 1.2).

One might begin a discussion of the piece with the sentence

Slow pieces in minor keys always make me feel sad.

But this alerts the reader to two unfortunate things:

- The author is more interested in his or her own opinions and feelings than in the work itself.
- An entire discussion is about to be based on a bland, naive, and highly personal statement.

Our author has thus broken one of the most basic rules of writing: *never make the reader doubt your ability.* A related situation occurs when a live performer inadvertently plants doubts in the mind of a listener through

EX. 1.2
Mozart, *Piano Concerto in A Major,* K. 488, II, opening.

inappropriate concert behavior, apparent nervousness, technical inaccuracies, or memory lapses. No one wants to feel insecure on another's behalf, so the instinct is to exit the performance out of embarrassment for the performer's predicament. The reader's mode of exit is to turn the page or put down the work altogether.

Yet the fact that the concerto movement is slow and in a minor key *is* relevant to the mood Mozart is trying to project, and our fictitious author's response may be close to that which Mozart intended. How, then, might we rewrite the sentence to use the obviously good instincts shown in the disastrous first version in a more effective and promising way? Perhaps:

> The second movement's slow tempo and minor key seem sad and poignant, particularly after the sweetness and brilliance of the first movement.

This version makes a similar point, but it offers musical evidence (that is, the comparison to what was heard immediately before) and it is put in a far less personal way. It speaks about the same melancholy musical effect, places it in the context of the previous movement, and uses as evidence what previously had been mere stimuli for authorial musings. Put this way, *it serves as proof:* almost any listener to Western concert and popular music knows, instinctively or from study, that minor keys and slow tempi frequently have, particularly in the eighteenth century, associations of sadness or drama.

A more detailed treatment of the opening might address the choice of F-sharp minor specifically, the harmonic language, the melodic intervals, the traditional associations of the underlying dance type (*siciliano*), and any number of other aspects, in order to strengthen the same point. But in most cases additional details would be unnecessary; two aspects of the music, clear and easy to hear, can be used to explain the listener's response. The fact that this response is not prefaced with "I feel that" and supported by "I just *hear* it that way," and that it is based on characteristics inherent in the music, makes it no less of an opinion, and no more a "fact." Opinion is present, but the reader knows that there is more support than authorial whim.

Because music is a nonverbal, largely nonrepresentative art, there sometimes seems to be little of a concrete nature about it, and it can prove to be a maddeningly elusive subject for an author. But we have seen that there are many ways to write about music, so there is no single right answer waiting to be discovered. What remains is to begin, and to begin without fear.

You are reading this book because of a commitment to music. This book will offer guidance, but you need to be reading indefatigably about music elsewhere and learning to identify good, meaningful, economical writing—writing upon which you can begin to model your own efforts. The same passion and drive that motivate you to practice, perform, compose, and teach music, or even just to listen to it and learn more about it, should also motivate you to improve your writing about it. Make it concise, make it elegant, make it compelling. Finally, be prepared to make mistakes. Mere avoidance of errors is no goal. Write freely, but self-evaluate brutally, and strive not to repeat your mistakes. The result will be writing that is gratifying both to read and to digest.

2

Writing about Music by and for Those Who Cannot (Necessarily) Read It

Most rock musicians lack formal musical training, and so do almost all rock commentators. They lack the vocabulary and techniques of musical analysis, and even the descriptive words that critics and fans do use—harmony, melody, riff, beat—are only loosely understood and applied. I share this ignorance . . . [1]

—SIMON FRITH

For most kinds of musical writing, it is highly desirable and always advantageous to be musically literate.[2] Whether one is writing reviews, publicity, or opinion, the technical knowledge of written musical language is irreplaceable. (Ideally, some performance experience—that is, rendering written musical symbols into living, breathing musical experiences—is highly desirable also.) The musically literate author is able to become a collaborator with the musical subject and can elucidate or respond to musical works and performances with collegial em-

---

[1]Simon Frith, *Sound Effects: Youth, Leisure, and the Politics of Rock 'N' Roll* (New York: Pantheon Books, 1982), 13.

[2]The ability to read music is an absolute requirement for the analysis and detailed discussion of musical content. This task will be addressed in Chapter 3.

21

pathy. The more experience a writer has with a subject, after all, the better informed the writing! Individuals with an ongoing commitment to effective writing about music must therefore seek musical instruction and experience, if they do not yet have it, so as to be fully prepared for the task.

Unarmed but overly ambitious authors require only a few words to embarrass themselves: "The album has a floating feeling. There is a high, motionless motion, and John shows his ability to play romance . . ."[3] Does the album *have* a floating feeling (do albums have feelings?) or is this how one listener felt upon hearing it? What *is* "motionless motion," anyway? Note also a tendency to be overly familiar, common in jazz and popular music writing, by referring to artists by their first names. In sum, the risk of writing something as windily meaningless as this description of jazz giant John Coltrane is simply too great to allow the wise writer to enter the ring unprepared.

That said, there are kinds of writing for which musical literacy is not a prerequisite. One kind of response to music's ability to excite the imagination consists of writing that utilizes elements of the fantastic. Consider the following passage from E. M. Forster's *Howards End,* in which the reader hears the close of Beethoven's Fifth Symphony through the ears of one of the characters:

> . . . as if things were going too far, Beethoven took hold of the goblins and made them do what he wanted. He appeared in person. He gave them a little push, and they began to walk in a major key instead of in minor, and then—he blew with his mouth, and they were scattered! Gusts of splendour, gods and demi-gods contending with vast swords, colour and fragrance broadcast on the field of battle, magnificent victory, magnificent death! . . . Any fate was titanic; any contest desirable; conqueror and conquered would alike be applauded by the angels of the utmost stars. . . .
>
> Beethoven chose to make all right in the end. He blew with his mouth for the second time, and again the goblins were scattered. He brought back the gusts of splendour, the heroism, the youth, the magnificence of life and of death, and, amid vast roarings of a superhuman joy, he led his Fifth Symphony to its conclusion. But the goblins were

---

[3]Cuthbert O. Simpkins, quoted in V. J. Panetta's review of Eric Nisenson's *Ascension: John Coltrane and His Quest, Notes* 52/1 (September 1995), 118.

there. They could return. He had said so bravely, and that is why one can trust Beethoven when he says other things.[4]

Writing such as this is best reserved for literature, not analysis or review. Nonetheless it illustrates how evocative nontechnical writing can be, and how subjective, untrained, and frankly emotional responses can suggest a musical mood or experience in a way that no amount of terminological precision can. As music itself is not usually composed with specialists in mind, such naive but impassioned reactions as that of Forster's character may well suggest successful, direct emotional communication of the kind many composers want to have with their listeners.

The use of imagery may also effectively set the stage for a more in-depth discussion. The following passage introduces a detailed treatment of a popular and accessible work by Johann Strauss. The encapsulation of its opening mood through a few everyday images is highly effective as an introduction to the detail of the later discussion of structure, musical materials, and compositional procedure.

> The first sounds we hear in Johann Strauss's *Emperor Waltz* are surely those of marching, rather than dancing, feet. The steady alternation—one, two, one, two—of soft string chords leads to a modest tune, its lightly military rhythm underlined by the rustle of the snare drum. Four bars in the woodwinds are answered by a pendant in the violins, then repeated in a slightly fuller setting (with the merest *soupçon* of a martial gesture from the trumpet), answered by a different pendant. Indubitably a march, but on a very special scale: perhaps a bird's-eye view of the parade ground, or toy soldiers at drill—the specific metaphor doesn't really matter, rather the sense of distance and of proportion that it conveys.[5]

No technical jargon (other than counting beats: one-two, one-two) is used here, and the musical character is clear and complete. Again, though, this is not an independent passage; it prepares the reader for the analysis that follows. While it ably illustrates a nontechnical approach, we need to ask what *self-standing* kinds of writing may successfully be done by those with no academic knowledge of music. For these authors, the potential vulnerabilities require a careful choice of circumstances.

---

[4]Edward Morgan Forster, *Howards End* [1910] (New York: Alfred A. Knopf, 1951), 40-41.

[5]David Hamilton, "The Secret Life of a Waltz," *High Fidelity* (October 1975), 36. Reprinted by permission.

WHAT YOU CAN AND CANNOT DO

The primary responsibility of any writer is to know what he or she is talking about. We tend to assume adequate preparation by the authors we read, and we are disappointed when, for example, musical terminology is misused. Words such as *form, harmony,* and *counterpoint* have explicit musical meanings that are not identical to their general meanings in nonmusical contexts. It is fair to say that if an author has no clear, specific understanding of how music works, then all analysis and use of musical terminology is off-limits. That author simply does not have the tools to complete the job, and will end up making a mess of it with pretentious and ignorant writing. Here is an example from a New York newspaper:

> Interwoven throughout Falla's music were the Phoenician modal effects of flamenco's 12-count *bulerias* on the symphonic line. Flamenco's *cante jondo* lived in [the singer's] voice as she transformed *El amor brujo* into an Andalusian creole. With [the dancer] embodying Falla's score, both women performed the intertext of Spanish and gypsy, paying homage to women performers in modernist style.[6]

This passage is prodigiously silly. The musical terms are randomly scrambled, followed by the ostentatious (and barely comprehending) change of tone to one of specialized academic criticism: *cante jondo* (deep song—a flamenco style) "living in" the singer's voice, the dancer's "embodying" Falla's score, "performing the intertext," and so on. Not only do the three clauses of the final sentence seem unrelated to one another, but "gypsy" remains uncapitalized—an ethnic insult in an effusive discussion of a style of music and dance in which Kalo Gypsies played a formative role. ("Roma" is preferable to "Gypsies," but it would require further discussion.)

It is thus apparent that musical detail, even in a nonanalytical context, is no area for novices. Because most people love music, many writers believe they can write about it on a technical level for which they are manifestly unequipped. The author with only general knowledge will not succeed when writing requires specificity of description and comprehension. In other words, if you do not thoroughly understand it, do not attempt to write about it.

What does this leave? Actually, a good deal.

---

[6]Ninotchka Bennahum, "Musical Modernismo," *The Village Voice,* April 1, 1997.

THE REACTION PAPER

The reaction paper, a staple of introductory music classes, is an excellent vehicle for organizing relatively unformed reactions to music and putting them into words. The attempt to produce coherent writing (it cannot be stated often enough) forces authors, from beginners to the most experienced, to refine and clarify our thoughts, draft by draft, before we expose them to our audience. Written after attendance at a live musical performance, the reaction paper enables the student-writer to put his or her reactions to the performance in clear form, and to demonstrate an understanding of musical concepts introduced in class and the course text through an informed response to the performance.

Here is a reaction paper written by a student in an Introduction to Music class who had just attended a performance of Puccini's opera *Tosca*. References to specific performers and places have been omitted.

TOSCA, by Giacomo Puccini

by Kristin L. Kremers

Tosca, an Italian opera written by Giacomo Puccini, premiered in Italy on January 14, 1900. The story is based upon Sardou's *La Tosca*. True to its genre of "tragic opera," it plays on your emotions and sweeps you up into the story. One gets an incredible feeling of fate being played out, and yet there is always that hope for things to work out in the end. *Tosca* has been a popular opera throughout history, and we are very fortunate to get the chance to see such an opera. This was my first opera attendance, and I must say I was very impressed. The combination of all the arts at their finest left quite an impression on me. Everything (the sets, performers, etc.) worked together in such a way that you just sat back and watched in awe.

First of all, I must admit that what impressed me the most were the sets. I was stunned and in disbelief at times by how complex and beautiful they were. They really set the mood with their 3-D effects and special lighting. For example, the Sant' Andrea Church's domed ceiling seemed awesomely real, and the effect of the stained glass shadow along with the Madonna painting was that of true devotion and the holiness of the place. In Act II, the use of the color red in the dungeon light, couch, Tosca's dress, etc. announced the presence of evil that seemed to emanate from the villain. The misty dawn in Act III foretold a dreary ending for all. My personal favorite, however, was the scene in which the guns fired, our hero falls, and the sky suddenly turns a deep scarlet. The color was so intense, it seemed to say "there is no turning back now." All throughout the opera the presence of Catholic objects of devotion (crosses, the Madonna, a statue of Gabriel) helped to play out the battle between good and evil.

One mustn't forget the importance of the singers of the opera, though. There were two guest singers: [X], a *spinto* soprano who played the heroine, opera singer Floria Tosca, and [Y], a tenor who played the hero, painter Mario Cavaradossi. They both sang beautifully, acting out the passion and drama of the opera marvelously. However, I did prefer Tosca's voice because she seemed a much stronger singer, as if nothing was going to prevent the person sitting in the top balcony, in the last row from hearing her sing. My favorite aria was Tosca's "Vissi d'arte" in the second act, sung as she lay on the ground. A shudder would go down my spine every time she would hit those high notes. The sudden change in pitches really created a dramatic effect. I was most impressed when Scarpia, played by [Z], sang his aria with the "Te Deum" chorus in the background. Although he seemed to be drowned out at times, the overall effect was quite powerful. You could feel the tension building up with the contrast of Scarpia's sacrilegious thoughts of Tosca and the piety of the parish.

The characters were cast very well. Tosca needed to be (and was) a strong woman with a dramatic soprano voice, and she was someone to be reckoned with. [A] was kind of skinny and small, fitting the part of the starved political prisoner Cesare Angelotti very well with his bass voice. The man who played Cavaradossi was well built, yet not huge and overpowering, with a good set of pipes. His tenor voice and stature helped him portray the "good guy." Best in my opinion was Scarpia, played by a large man with a booming baritone voice that could easily intimidate and be seen as sinister.

A beautiful part of the opera was the orchestra. Their playing set the mood, foretelling the events that were to happen. There seemed to be certain instruments associated with major characters. The flute and woodwind instruments portrayed Tosca, the strings were for Cavaradossi, the horns for Scarpia. An especially memorable moment was when the harp signalled the coming of dawn in Act III.

As far as the language it was sung in, I am glad it was in English rather than Italian. The fact that it was in English helped during my first opera experience because it allowed a deeper understanding of what was happening. The length of *Tosca* was just right. It was neither too long so that I got bored, nor too short to complete the story.

I loved attending the opera *Tosca*. It was a positive and educational, as well as a very entertaining, experience for me. I would gladly go again to hear, see, and take in all that the opera has to offer with its combination of the arts at their finest.

This paper, clearly and concisely written, demonstrates that a good deal of learning took place before the opera began. It also demonstrates that the author enjoyed herself—a good thing but by no means a necessary one—and that she gained a good deal from the performance. She shows an awareness of all the components of an operatic production (music, literature, drama, lighting design, sets, and costumes), the genre of this particular opera (tragedy), and the plot. Individual moments are singled out for their effectiveness: the female lead's rendition of one aria, another aria performed while a religious piece is being sung simultaneously in the background, a particular lighting cue. Ms. Kremers addresses many aspects of this opera, from individual performances to the symbolism inherent in the set design and the multifaceted nature of the artwork as a whole, in an unaffected, highly readable paper that gives no evidence of previous musical experience, much less musical literacy.

One could still suggest improvements, pointing out that Scarpia's feelings for Tosca are lustful rather than "sacrilegious" and citing phrases or devices that are too informal for written prose: "it plays on your emotions and sweeps you up into the story," the reference to the tenor's "good pipes," the overuse of contractions. But the writing, while entirely nontechnical, is clear, colorful, and it gives a good picture of the performance in question and what the author got out of it. It is evident that a great deal of learning took place.

THE CONCERT REVIEW

The reaction paper, consisting mostly of first impressions but founded on prior academic preparation, is related to another kind of "morning after" writing: the concert review. While every musician dreads a review by the musically inexperienced writer, musical experience need not necessarily involve musical literacy. One can maintain a lifetime's interest in music, with a long history of concert attendance and a large collection of recordings, perhaps even singing in a church or community choir and playing in folk-music groups, and still not have acquired musical literacy. The fundamental issues in review writing have to do with the reviewer's audience, goals, intent, and morality. The best preparation for reviewing, especially the reviewing of classical concerts, is a knowledge of and experience with the repertoire being performed. Mere musical literacy is no guarantee of this. Indeed, it can often mislead a reviewer into thinking he or she knows more than may be the case. What, before we go further, is the purpose of a concert review? It is multifaceted, and its focus depends on the publication in which it appears (or the nature of the assignment) and its audience.

Reporting on a News Event

Musicians almost universally regard concert reviews with suspicion and hostility, often on the basis of bad personal experience. But in most situations, a primary function of the review is reportage, informing the readership of a newspaper or magazine about an arts event that took place in the community. Relatively few communities have an individual with advanced musical expertise who is willing or able to write *what* the newspaper editor wants, *when* he or she wants it (that is, late the same evening that the concert takes place), for the available amount of money (usually negligible). Accordingly, many concert reviews are written by people whose chief qualification is a general interest in the arts. Such reviews may consist of discussion of the works performed, some evaluation of the performers, and description of the general effect upon audience and reviewer. Given the nature of both writer and audience, the question of tone is all-important.

In most places, concert music and the other arts are supported by a small minority. Accordingly, a spirit of appreciation, with the idea of inspiring broader interest in music in general, is an appropriate starting point for the reviewer. It is an unhappy fact that certain reviewers, taking advantage of the fact that their words will be read in the following day's newspaper, relish sitting in merciless judgment on the musicians they review. No example of this destructive and entirely inappropriate writing is needed here; its character is unmistakable.

This is not to say that performers never deserve censure. Even under the most stressful and irregular performing circumstances, the audience must be respected, regardless of excessive coughing or applause at inappropriate times. When issues of competence or professionalism are raised—say, if the technical flaws in a performance multiply to the point of eclipsing all other aspects, or if a performer shows disdain for the audience or other performers—then it is the responsibility of the reviewer not to soft-pedal these aspects, which after all lie at the heart of artistic communication. Initial goodwill in the reviewer need not, in this unfortunate circumstance, become a governing principle or requirement. The performer has earned, by charging admission for a musical performance but not executing professional responsibilities, whatever rebuke the reviewer has to offer. Fortunately, such cases are rare.

The best mindset for reviewers is a positive and appreciative one that brings a benignly neutral attitude to each performance.

Artistic Evaluation

Going beyond simple reportage, why would one evaluate a musical performance? For precisely the same reasons one would review a movie or play: so that those not present may have some idea of what was missed, and so that they may consider attending performances by the same performers (or of the same works, or of works by the same composers). Artistic evaluation examines the components of the performance, which include technical mastery, interpretive concept, style awareness, and the ability to communicate and move the audience. Each of these is, to some extent, subjective: technical mastery is obvious on a basic level, but beyond that level, criteria can be highly individual; an interpretive concept may be obvious to one listener and mystifying to another (and it can be a matter of taste); style awareness is a matter of informed debate; and the ability to communicate with a listener is ultimately a personal judgment. A reviewer cannot pretend to speak for others' perceptions, regardless of how representative of the readership he or she feels, but still should not write from a position too distant from that of most of the readership. Matters of precise musical detail are best left for scholarly articles and conversation among musicians. Treating such specifics in a review is impractical and therefore inadvisable.

A good writer is nonetheless able to convey a great deal of information about a performer's artistry using nontechnical language, and in doing so to communicate to readers on a variety of levels. Take this excerpt from Virgil Thomson's review of the cellist Pierre Fournier's American debut in New York (the review appeared in the *New York Herald* on November 14, 1948):

> Excellence in the technical handling of the cello is always primarily a matter of avoiding pitfalls. Mr. Fournier does not let his instrument groan or scratch or squeak or buzz, and yesterday he did not miss exact pitch on more than just a very few notes. Neither did he at any time force his tone beyond the volume of optimum sonority. His sound, in consequence, was always pleasant and, thanks to Mr. Fournier's fine musical sensitivity, extremely varied.
>
> That sensitivity was present in positive form, moreover, as liveness of rhythm and in the wonderful shaping and shading of each line and phrase. Many cellists can play with dignity and style, as Mr. Fournier did, an unaccompanied Bach suite; but few can play a Brahms sonata, as he did yesterday the F major, with such buoyancy and spontaneity, such grace of feeling and no heaviness at all. I know of none who can match him in the Debussy Sonata.
>
> This work is rather a rhapsody than a sonata in the classical sense, and yet it needs in execution a sonata's continuous flow and long-line

planning. It needs also the utmost of delicacy and of variety in coloration and a feeling of freedom in its rhythmic progress. Its performance yesterday by Mr. Fournier and his accompanist, George Reeves, was a high point in a season already notable for good ensemble work . . . [7]

There is not one sentence in this excerpt, from those addressing technical mastery, the shaping and shading of phrases, or interpretive flow and long-line planning, that would not be comprehensible to any music lover, whether musically literate or not. Of course, Virgil Thomson, an important twentieth-century American composer and music critic, was musically literate. But in the reviewing process, one is rarely called upon to display one's learning, and Thomson does not. He looks for the best, in this review, and is not disappointed. Moreover, he honors the collaborating artist by acknowledging him by name (which is *always* the right thing to do) rather than equating him with the stage crew by leaving him nameless.

Here is another example, by Dawn Kummer, an undergraduate violin student, who reviews a faculty composition concert. She focuses not on the performance but on the work, a work she has never heard before, and in describing the interaction between musical and nonmusical media she leaves her own learning aside and gives a good sense of the work as a whole while using little or no technical terminology.

This program had two highlights. The first was *Images From the Edge of Time* by John McLaird, a piece inspired by pictures sent back to Earth by the Hubble space telescope. McLaird compiled these images into three short segments of film, then wrote the music to accompany them. Although the music could stand on its own, I greatly enjoyed the visual as well as the aural experience. The first segment was titled "Galaxies and Stars." The music was busy sounding, with many rapidly-moving passages. It perfectly matched images bursting with light and color. The

---

[7]Virgil Thomson, from "Virtuoso Makes Music," which originally appeared on November 14, 1948. It is reprinted in Thomson, *Music Right and Left* (New York: Henry Holt and Company, 1951), 43.

second was "Novae and Nebulae: The Birth and Death of Stars."
The music here was slower and more solemn, befitting the wonder
and gravity of the subject. The final segment, "Images From the
Edge of Time: Pictures of Different Objects," was more
contrapuntal. This piece was written for full orchestra, although its
performance here was entirely synthesized. Except for the
extremes of range (especially in the last movement), the difference
was barely noticeable.

Ms. Kummer's description touches on a variety of aspects of the piece, including the inspiration for its composition, the multimedia approach taken by the composer, the musical contrasts between the three movements, and the performing forces, both as conceived and as realized in this particular performance. The only specifically musical concepts here are range and contrapuntal texture, which would be familiar to any music appreciation student. The result is that her writing would make sense to virtually any reader.

In brief, although music literacy is desirable in writing concert reviews, without it a great deal may still be communicated. Far more important for the reviewing process are perceptive listening and a firm understanding of one's audience and the kind of information they will be prepared to understand.

Promoting Community Interest in Music

To promote a community's interest in music is an important goal of many concert reviews, particularly those written in places that are not urban musical centers, and it would be disingenuous to act as if only higher artistic considerations were relevant. Of this promotional aspect, little need be said other than to reassure reviewers that they need not sacrifice authorial integrity. Putting live musical activity in a favorable light (or in as favorable a light as possible) will in most cases serve the greater good: more community awareness of, and interest in, live music. Enumerating a performer's technical flaws or questionable interpretive decisions will not advance this goal, and positive aspects of a performance should receive the most attention. This is not to say that the review should be mere publicity fluff; it is simply advisable to remember that focusing on the positive will best serve the greater purpose. A positive outlook will be far preferable, for a local audience, to bitter criticism of local artists or anecdotes of higher standards in urban centers. Always remember for whom you write, and why.

POPULAR AND WORLD MUSICS

There is little agreement on the amount of formal training needed to write about popular music and about world music. ("World music" denotes both the traditional—that is, folk—musics of the world and the "classical" or art musics of cultures outside the West.) Popular and world musics are in some ways parallel. On the one hand, both repertories are part of the everyday experiences of millions of musically nonliterate people, and often the performers themselves can neither read nor write music, so it would seem odd to require musical literacy and academic training for those writing about such music. On the other hand, there is a degree of ethnocentricity in the position that Western classical music somehow requires potential authors to have a kind of background that popular and world musics do not. Obviously, Western musical literacy is relevant especially for Western classical music, but there are many who believe that thorough academic training is necessary to write responsibly about *any* music, that there is neither inherent irony nor contradiction in enjoying far more training than your musical subject. The real answer lies with each individual case: the amount of training the author needs will depend on what specifically about the music is to be discussed.

The quotation from Simon Frith that heads this chapter makes an important point. Frith is one of England's most prominent rock writers, and his statement about many rock musicians' lack of technical vocabulary is certainly true. (A case in point is ex-Beatle Paul McCartney, a fine electric bassist, one of the most famous songwriters in history, and more recently a composer of concert music. Until at least the early 1990s he was musically illiterate.) Frith, a sociologist, tends to address rock music's place in society, the elements of listeners' culture and collective psyche it touches, and the commercial aspects of the rock market. For these subjects, musical literacy is unnecessary, as it would probably be in similar discussions relating to classical music. To expect more of authors and readers than of the musicians themselves, in such cases, seems pointlessly elitist—a latter-day echo of the Roman author Boethius, who felt that the only true musicians were judges and critics, while the performers and composers who made the music were little more than slaves and artisans.

A passage from Edward Macan's discussion of the album *Tarkus,* by the progressive-rock band Emerson, Lake and Palmer, illustrates how much can be communicated without academic terminology.

> The most impressive musical achievement of *Tarkus* is the effective tension maintained between impetuous, improvisatory sections and coherent long-range planning. Besides effectively juxtaposing different approaches to tempo, instrumentation, and harmony, *Tarkus* also makes effective use of contrasts in melodic character; the rhythmically smooth, stepwise vocal lines of the second and sixth movements can be contrasted with the jagged, rhythmically irregular motives of movements one, three, and five or the short, incantatory themes of the movements four and seven. Contrasts in meter play a role as well, since the instrumental movements tend toward unusual meters (the first and third movements are in five), while the "song" movements are all in common time (i.e., four).[8]

Macan, writing a book for a nonspecialist audience, here provides an overview of the pacing of the album as a whole. He compares the various movements with regard to melodic language (conjunct or "stepwise" melody being a basic concept), rhythmic character, and meter (for which the only technical knowledge required is the ability to count beats and sense accents). Macan, a trained musicologist, is of course literate, but music literacy is unnecessary for the audience he seeks to reach.

That said, it is also undeniable that rock songs (like other artworks, popular and otherwise) often require specialized terminology for their explanation and discussion, and whether or not the artist would understand that terminology is irrelevant. An example of this is the excerpt from Matthew Brown's analysis of Jimi Hendrix's song "Little Wing," which appears in Chapter 3; precise knowledge of musical terminology and the ability to mentally "hear" chord progressions are prerequisites for understanding the writing. While the music is fairly nontraditional (academically speaking, at least), the discussion is squarely within standard analytical boundaries, and comprehension of it is virtually impossible without full music literacy.

Depending on the author's point, the reader's need for academic background can go beyond basic musical training. Consider Robert

---

[8]Edward Macan, *Rocking the Classics* (New York and Oxford: Oxford University Press, 1997), 94.

Walser's critical commentary on the song "Heaven Sent," by the heavy metal band Dokken:

> The guitar solo, often the site of virtuosic transcendence of a metal song's constructions of power and control, is, in "Heaven Sent," a veritable catalog of the musical semiotics of doom. As with "ground bass" patterns in seventeenth-century opera, the harmonic pattern uses cyclicism to suggest fatefulness; as in certain of Bach's keyboard pieces, the virtuoso responds to the threat of breakdown with irrational, frenzied chromatic patterns. The guitar solo is an articulation of frantic terror, made all the more effective by its technical impressiveness and its imitations of vocal sounds such as screams and moans. After the solo, the song's chorus intensifies these images through ellision [sic]: seven measures long instead of the normal, balanced eight, the pattern cycles fatalistically, without rest or resolution.[9]

Such concepts as elided seven-bar phrases, chromaticism, and ground basses are probably foreign to readers who have not had systematic music study, and the comparisons with seventeenth-century opera and Bach's keyboard works would elude many who have not studied music history. Beyond that, Walser draws heavily on the vocabulary of cultural criticism. Such ideas as "the constructions of power and control" and "the semiotics of doom" are likely to puzzle readers who do not make it a point to keep abreast of contemporary academic critical discourse. In sum, this kind of writing is targeted at a specific, relatively narrow audience (that is, academics with an interest in music); those without musical training and a good deal of experience with academic discourse are simply not equipped to understand this kind of cross-disciplinary approach.

World musics—traditional and cultivated alike—pose problems similar to those of popular music. A typical assignment in world music courses is the basic exploratory paper, which might address the musical instruments and the musical language of another culture, and the uses and situation of music within that culture. For this (and depending on the depth of the inquiry), musical literacy may not be necessary. An author can provide an overview of a foreign music and its instruments without

---

[9]Robert Walser, *Running with the Devil: Power, Gender, and Madness in Heavy Metal Music* (Hanover, NH and London: Wesleyan University Press, 1993), 119.

providing in-depth analysis and musical examples. Indeed, the ethnomusicologist Bruno Nettl observes:

> The world's tribal musical cultures . . . have less in the way of music theory and of professionalization of musicians, and they have no musical notation. Quantitatively, their musics are simpler than the art musics of the world.[10]

This observation (which Nettl follows with the counterexample of African rhythmic structures) will only go so far. It may briefly reassure an author with no musical literacy, but musical literacy itself may be largely irrelevant to the musical culture in question. All musicians acknowledge the gap between musical notation and the music *itself* that notation seeks to record, or that is realized from it; while this gap is perceived to be large in Western classical music, for most other musics it is incomparably greater.

Our reliance on our inherited form of notation weights our understanding of music in favor of those aspects that are readily notatable, and it places those that are less so at a substantial disadvantage. Richard Middleton illustrates this shaping of our musical thought and perception in his identification of the difficulties in applying standard musical vocabulary to popular music. Since Western art music is notation-based, our terminology enables us to talk best about such aspects of music as harmony and meter, but it puts us at a disadvantage when we discuss

> non-standard pitch and non-discrete pitch movement (slides, slurs, blue notes, microtones, and so on); irregular, irrational rhythms, polyrhythms, and rhythmic nuance (off-beat phrasing, slight delays, anticipations and speed-ups, and the complex durational relationships often involved in heterophonic and 'loose' part-playing, and overlapping antiphonal phrases); nuances of ornamentation, accent, articulation (attack, sustain, decay: what electronic musicians and sound engineers call the 'envelope') and performer idiolect; specificities (as opposed to abstractions) of timbre . . . [11]

---

[10]Bruno Nettl, *Folk and Traditional Music of the Western Continents* [1965] (Englewood Cliffs, NJ: Prentice-Hall, 1990), 1-2.

[11]Richard Middleton, *Studying Popular Music* (Philadelphia: Open University Press, 1990), 104-05.

Even full Western musical literacy, then, does not necessarily equip an author to write easily about many aspects of popular music. The same is true—only more so—of world musics, which potentially have completely different theoretical (codified or not), practical, pedagogical, and aesthetic principles. Does a responsible author attempt to write about Indian classical music without a solid knowledge of what a *raga* is, or about Arabic music without a knowledge of the *maqam?* Does a knowledge of Western musical theory allow us to discuss the many subtle ways in which music, in many cultures, is understood to connect this world and the spirit realm? How can we engage in a comprehensible discussion of the specifics of a music that cannot practically be adapted to our notational system?

For these musics, authors need training of a different kind, perhaps (or perhaps not) involving musical notation—that of Western music or any other kind. What will almost certainly be necessary, however, is an understanding of the conceptual background and vocabulary of relevant cultural studies and anthropology, and they lie far beyond the scope of this book.

The distinction between general, introductory writing and more detailed, informed writing is an important one. The former may be done without a substantial amount of prior training, but the latter requires it. The question of context mentioned at the beginning of this section thus remains: while is it wrong to imagine that someone without Western music literacy will be able to write anything of value about popular or world musics, it is also a mistake to think that these musics, because of (in some cases) their relative simplicity or (in others) their remoteness from Western conceptions, may safely be written about without sufficient preparation and experience.

To summarize this chapter, the kinds of writing that may successfully be done without the benefit of music literacy include:

- literary impressions
- reviews
- response papers
- *certain kinds* of writing about primarily oral traditions (rock, world musics, etc.), but with the greatest possible care

To this list may be added other kinds of writing addressed elsewhere in this book:

- press releases
- article summaries and abstracts, given sufficient comprehension

The primary requirements for writing about music are clear listening and thinking, knowledge of one's audience, and an awareness of one's own limitations. For those intending ongoing activity in this area, acquiring music literacy and systematic music training are necessary. For those branching into non-Western musics, the culture and type of music will define the academic preparation needed.

3

Writing Music Analysis

*In all compositions I endeavor to fathom the diverse impulses
inspiring them and their inner life. Is not this much more interesting
than the game of pulling them to pieces, like curious watches?[1]*
—M. CROCHE THE DILETTANTE HATER
[CLAUDE DEBUSSY]

ANALYSIS AND ITS USES

I know of no more accurate or helpful definition of analysis than that of
Ian Bent, from *The New Grove Dictionary of Music and Musicians:*

> The primary impulse of analysis is an empirical one: to get to grips
> with something on its own terms rather than in terms of other things.
> Its starting-point is a phenomenon itself rather than external factors
> (such as biographical facts, political events, social conditions, educa-
> tional methods and all the other factors that make up the environment
> of that phenomenon). . . .
>
> Analysis is the means of answering directly the question "How does
> it work?".[2]

This is a traditionalist view. That is, many contemporary scholars
would argue that the question "How does it work?" is incompletely answered when biographical facts, social conditions, and so on remain out-

---

[1]Claude Debussy, *Monsieur Croche the Dilettante Hater* [1905], in *Three
Classics in the Aesthetic of Music* (New York: Dover, 1962), 5.

[2]Ian Bent, "Analysis," *The New Grove Dictionary of Music and Musicians,*
ed. Stanley Sadie (London: Macmillan, 1980), vol. 1, 342.

side the discussion; they do, after all, have direct bearing on the way listeners hear and understand music—and therefore on "how it works." But as Bent's definition stands, it addresses the workings of the piece itself, the way the musical materials are deployed and how they interrelate. This is precisely how analysis is usually understood.

Why analyze? Does this endeavor represent no more than disassembling musical works "like curious watches," as Debussy contemptuously suggested? Pulling music apart is a necessary part of analysis, but it is only the first step. The ability to think analytically about music is an absolute necessity for those who seek to understand, teach, interpret, and write about music, and—properly done—analysis has far more to do with "fathoming music's inner life" than it does with disassembly. Our primary concern is *writing* analysis; the analytical skills themselves must be learned in music theory and history courses.

Most analysis depends upon printed score examples, as does the following discussion of the opening of the first movement of Mozart's piano concerto in A major, K. 488 (shown in Example 3.1).

> The subtle poignancy of the g-natural in bar 1 is a master-stroke, as is the clash between g-sharp and a in the 4th beat of bar 2, and the less

EX. 3.1
Mozart, *Piano Concerto in A Major*, K. 488, I, opening (piano reduction).

obvious dissonance between the chord of A major and the d in the bass in bar 4. It is these moments of harmonic tension that prevent the music from being merely bland; behind the sunny façade there are shadowy places.[3]

This excerpt from a longer analysis addresses how the passage "works" not by describing everything that happens, a good deal of which is obvious from the musical example, but rather by identifying those aspects that are noteworthy and that contribute to a unique effect: the unexpected harmony ($^V7/_{iv}$) caused by the G-natural, and the dissonances that follow in bars 2 and 4. The analyst expects the reader to understand the eighteenth-century harmonic grammar in the musical example, but otherwise he offers no jargon or advanced analytical concepts. Some might find such figurative ideas as "poignancy," "sunny façade," and "shadowy places" to be outside the realm of pure analysis, but since they anchor Mozart's compositional choices to the way many hear and understand his music, their relevance to "how it works" is apparent. Analysis does not consist of simply listing characteristics or identifying particular gestures in a score example; it must show how these gestures relate to one another, how they work together to produce a composite effect and contribute to a coherent whole.

Analyses are often done in accordance with a specific system, such as traditional harmonic analysis, the linear analysis of Heinrich Schenker (illustrated by a characteristic kind of graphic representation[4]), or set theory. In each system, certain guidelines and analytical vocabulary are established at the outset, and the musical information is then interpreted within that context. Alternatively, analyses may be eclectic in approach, adhering to no particular model but seeking to clarify by whatever means seem appropriate. A certain amount of terminology is common to virtually all analytical approaches, so a solid background in music theory, in addition to complete musical literacy, is a prerequisite for both understanding and writing musical analyses.

---

[3]Antony Hopkins, *Talking About Concertos* (London: Heinemann Educational Books, 1964), 25.

[4]Examples of Schenker's own analytical work may be found in Heinrich Schenker, *Five Graphic Musical Analyses* [1933], ed. Felix Salzer (New York: Dover, 1969). Example 3.4 also gives a Schenker graph.

ANALYTICAL CONTENT VS. PLAY-BY-PLAY

Example 3.2 gives the opening of the vocal part of Franz Schubert's famous *Der Hirt auf dem Felsen* (*The Shepherd on the Rock*) for voice, piano, and obbligato clarinet, op. 129 (D. 965).

As was the case with the Mozart analysis excerpted above, the presence of the musical example obviates the need for lengthy description, and the explanation of "how it works" can be focused on those aspects that are interesting or atypical. More obvious features may be pointed out when there is reason to do so, but they need not be described or explained. A treatment of this short passage might run this way:

> Noteworthy, here, is Schubert's treatment of the text. The opening line of the poem, "Wenn auf dem höchsten Fels ich steh" ("When I stand on the highest cliff"), is set to a stable piano accompaniment with unchanging texture and tonic-dominant harmonies. The melody here makes use of word-painting: the "highest cliff" is suggested not only by the two isolated high f pitches but also by the disjunct "climbing" figures that lead up to them.

The analyst has chosen to address the text-music relationship, which is central to any understanding of vocal music and in this case is particularly instructive. Other approaches might begin by commenting on the almost exclusive use of chord tones in the melody, or on its wide range, or on aspects of the rhythm and harmony. But the inclusion of a musical example enables the author to keep description to a minimum and to proceed to identifying important points. The cumulative effect is one of per-

EX. 3.2
Schubert, *Der Hirt auf dem Felsen*, mm. 38-42.

suasion; the writer explains how the passage works using analytical arguments supported by reference to the score.

What will not pass for analysis is what I call play-by-play. Play-by-play, more a sign of inexperience than anything else, is frequently produced for a student's first analysis assignment. It consists of detailed, literal narrative of what the notes are doing in a particular passage. A play-by-play treatment of the Schubert excerpt seen above in Ex. 3.2 might read this way:

> The melody, in $\frac{3}{4}$ time, begins on the upbeat with a dotted-eighth-note d and sixteenth-note e♭, a figure which leads up to a half-note f on the downbeat of the following bar. A descending triplet b♭ arpeggio on the third beat (d-b♭-f) leads down to a dotted-quarter-note d downbeat on the bar, after which, following an eighth-note f above, it ascends back up to the same high f through another arpeggiating triplet (this time, b♭-f-d). The phrase ends with an ornamental triplet on the third beat (e♭-f-d) that comes to rest on a c half-note below, on the following downbeat. The piano accompaniment is static—downbeat left-hand octaves followed by triplet chords in the right hand—and the harmony is equally unremarkable, consisting of two bars of the tonic followed by two of the dominant.

This passage is about twice as long as the previous passage, says far less, and consists entirely of a narration of musical events. While such a description is not necessarily an evil, it needs to lead somewhere, which this example does not—it only duplicates the information found in the musical example. Note that without a musical example, this kind of writing is still tedious and thankless: few readers will have the patience or the ability to visualize or hum the line in their heads while they are reading. It is far better to listen to the piece. Because following an analysis is never an effortless task, the author must write concisely, clearly, and meaningfully, and do everything possible to facilitate understanding. Experience shows that play-by-play descriptions do not fulfill these goals.

It is true that play-by-play has often been used in writing notes for recordings and concert programs. The assumption in such cases is that the listener is about to listen to the music under discussion, so the guidance of a play-by-play description is appropriate. In my opinion, there are far better ways to write such annotations; this task is discussed in Chapter 4.

One caveat: a detailed play-by-play treatment of a particular passage may be necessary to establish, for purposes of the ensuing explanation, the precise nature of the musical elements or compositional choices. This is standard procedure for major analyses, where an initial musical description will provide the fuel for pages of discussion. But for most student analyses, valuable space should not be devoted to material easily gleaned from a musical example.

Finally, valuable as musical examples are, it is necessary to be judicious in their use; pages of score excerpts should not be allowed to swamp the explanation. Too many examples can produce an effect analogous to too many charts or graphs: the reader becomes impatient with having to jump repeatedly between the text and the accompanying music, and the thread of the argument becomes increasingly difficult to follow. A balance between explanatory words and illustrative musical examples, with a cold eye to the economical use of both, will point the way to effective analytical writing. (For information on how to incorporate musical examples in a manuscript, see Chapter 8.)

Analysis Without Musical Examples

Certain kinds of analysis do not require musical examples. Rock and many world musics are not notation-based (though they can certainly be notated), and it is not always helpful to render into notation, for purposes of analysis, what was not notated in any precise way in the first place. This passage from Matthew Brown's discussion of Jimi Hendrix's song "Little Wing" does not require an example:

> Most significantly, Hendrix's melodic and harmonic idiom also shows strong psychedelic influences. Whereas bars 1-4 are built from the familiar blues progression I-III-IV-I, bars 5-10 have quite different origins. For one thing, the overall motion from a B-minor chord (m. 5) through a C-major sonority (m. 8) to a D-major chord (mm. 9-10) is not typical of a blues in E; progressions of this type, with their weak tonal functions, are far more common in rock.[5] For another, the chromatic chords on B-flat and F in measures 5 and 7 are idiomatic of psychedelic music; both chords lie outside the prevailing pentatonic collection.

---

[5]Author's footnote: Richard Bobbitt, *Harmonic Technique in the Rock Idiom* (Belmont, CA: Wadsworth, 1976), 92-110.

Lastly, many of Hendrix's voicings are decidedly unbluesy. Most striking in this regard are the ubiquitous 4-3 and 9-8 suspensions and stacked fifths.[6]

Without relying on a musical example, Brown produces a clear, coherent analytical passage targeted at a musically trained readership. He uses standard musical terminology to discuss Hendrix's harmonic language, and while the reader may understand the differences between blues, rock, and psychedelic music, Brown explains his observations anyway. To understand this passage, it is necessary that the reader be able to "hear" a I-III-IV-I harmonic progression, and one from B minor to C to D; to understand how 4-3 and 9-8 suspensions work; and to know what stacked fifths and a pentatonic collection are. Musically trained readers who have some experience with rock music will be capable of "hearing" the music and understanding the discussion, but it is still true (and somewhat paradoxical) that musical analyses such as this, which do not use examples, require more of the reader than those that do.

Technical Terminology

The Hendrix analysis above illustrates that, whether a musical example is presented or not, you will need to use a certain amount of specific, technical vocabulary. Do not revel unnecessarily in technical language, but do not take heroic measures to avoid it; readers of musical analyses should be expected to understand it. For many general readers, concepts from undergraduate-level harmony class, such as Phrygian cadences and parallel fifths (or dominant chords and dotted rhythms), will be incomprehensible. The same goes, only more so, for terms such as background, middleground, and foreground, and for references to numbered pitch collections such as 014 trichords. Yet Schenker-based analysis is pointless without the former, and set theory depends on the latter. One of the main goals of classroom analysis is to demonstrate mastery of new concepts and vocabulary. Soft-pedaling such vocabulary and taking time and space for definitions are often counterproductive.

---

[6]Matthew Brown, "'Little Wing': A Study in Musical Cognition," in John Covach and Graeme M. Boone, eds., *Understanding Rock: Essays in Musical Analysis* (New York and Oxford: Oxford University Press, 1997), 163.

Needlessly obscure prose is always wrong, but precise technical terminology is necessary in musical analysis. When you are writing musical analysis, you are *not* writing for the general reader.

Two Analytical Excerpts with Commentary

In explaining the nature of analysis, strong models will serve better than directives and proscriptions. This excerpt from Leonard Ratner's *Classic Music* discusses the opening of Haydn's piano sonata in E-flat major, Hob. XVI:52:

> Haydn's subtle and eccentric rhetoric asserts itself immediately; the first two measures represent a cadence, a complete statement anchored to a tonic pedal point. This is a powerful gesture, but it is very short, too short for even the briefest of normal periods. To extend it, Haydn uses an echo, itself varied and re-echoed again and again until it gathers momentum to become an agent for continuation in m. 5. The melody arrives at the tonic for the first time at m. 6; we could easily imagine a dominant under the descending parallel thirds in the second half of m. 5, so that the tonic of m. 6 could represent an authentic cadence and the end of the period. But Haydn changes the sense of the tonic twice: first, by underpinning it with C so that a deceptive cadence is suggested; second, by completing the chord with an A♭ so that the harmony becomes IV⁶. At this point, the sixth chord is defined as the carrier of the *stile legato* action, continuing the descent that it began with the first echo. The period ends with a *Tacterstickung* in m. 9, where the tonic serves a double function—arrival and departure. Again the peremptory brevity of the opening figure, always presenting in a two-measure phrase, provides a springboard for contrasting action; this time, the tirata heard in m. 1 becomes a brilliant-style flourish, and the bound style, instead of being the *final* consequence of the echo, enters early to rob the cesura of the march figure of its final beat. Throughout the movement, the passage in *stile legato* is treated in a flexible manner; it may enter upon a first, second, third, or fourth beat; it may be 8 to 21 beats in length.[7]

Example 3.3 gives the musical excerpt, the opening of the first movement of Haydn's most famous piano sonata. Such concepts as parallel

---

[7]Leonard G. Ratner, *Classic Music: Expression, Form, and Style* (New York: Schirmer, 1980), 413.

EX. 3.3
Haydn, *Sonata in E-flat Major* (H.V. XVI:52), I, opening.

thirds, tonic and dominant, and deceptive and authentic cadences are familiar to anyone who has taken a year of tonal theory, and they need no definition in an analysis of this kind. *Tacterstickung* (a German term meaning "the suppression of a measure"), *stile legato* (not legato articulation, but "bound style," a reference to the suspensions in the tenor voice, which changes its pitch a quarter-note after the bass and soprano voices in mm. 6-7), and other terms will not be immediately understood by every music student, but Ratner has explained them earlier in his book. Elements are identified with each other and with fulfilling specific roles:

for example, the repeated echo mentioned in the third sentence of the analysis serves both to expand a too-short opening period to a usable length and, once it takes on a life of its own, to serve as an agent for continuation. Ratner's analysis, which here concerns itself primarily with compositional choices in harmony, phrase structure, and surface musical gesture, uses a minimum of jargon yet addresses a range of advanced concepts.

Let us now examine a longer, more detailed excerpt, one that does not shy away from detail or technical terminology. This excerpt, a discussion of a transitional passage from Gershwin's *Rhapsody in Blue,* is taken from Steven Gilbert's book-length analytical study of Gershwin's music.

In short, *Rhapsody in Blue* is not nearly as rhapsodic as it may first seem. Its themes are joined by a multiplicity of motivic relationships. It has a coherent fundamental structure. Where it does appear to meander somewhat, it does so in a controlled way. The processes whereby this control is achieved are central to Gershwin's compositional technique. One is the recursive harmonic progression, which gives the illusion of motion to passages that begin and end in the same place (such as the succession of minor thirds from G to G that is the harmonic basis for the opening of part 2). The other is the transitional passage, a device for which Gershwin, for better or worse, has become well known.

Two such passages make their initial appearance early in part 1. The first, transition 1, begins at R4+6 [Example 3.4] and leads to the A-major entrance of main theme 1 at R4+14, or three bars before R5. Though harmonically static, its upper voices provide considerable interest from the standpoint of both the small and larger dimensions. The initial three measures comprise an ascending sequence supporting the top voice e^2-f^2-g^2, whose vertical cross-sections are each based on the corresponding dominant seventh. The descending portion also begins on an E7 chord with e^2 in the top voice, whose notes alternate with their upper neighbors (diatonic in the first three bars, chromatic in the fourth), creating a whole-tone scale of semitonal dyads. In the fourth measure (whose immediate repetition is not shown), the emphasis shifts from the first to the second note of each dyad, then shifts back at the measure's end.

The larger significance of the upper voices is identical with the underpinning of the entire passage—namely, the dominant of A. The resolution of this dominant provides the clue to the larger melodic progression beamed in Example [3.4]: from e^2 (the starting pitch) to d^1 (the registrally displaced passing seventh, unfolding to $g\sharp$) to $c\sharp^2$. The

EX. 3.4
Gershwin, *Rhapsody in Blue*, Schenkerian graph of transition beginning in m. R4+6.

latter, the resolution of the passing seventh, is absorbed into an inner voice by virtue of the overlapped entrance of main theme 1.[8]

The second of these three paragraphs is not light reading, but I see no way for it to be further clarified or simplified. Gilbert's identification of the melodic implications of the passage (e^2-f^2-g^2 in the first three bars, followed by descending half-step pairs a whole step apart), the harmonic content (dominant seventh chords on the pitches c, f, and g, etc.), and the harmonic implications (it remains on the dominant throughout, despite the suggestion of departure and arrival) is well put, understandable, and above all economical. Even so, it may require several readings to keep track of what is going on—which is not uncommon in specialized writing in any field (think of explanations of mathematical formulae, for example). But notice that a context for this material has been prepared by the first paragraph, which deals with the *Rhapsody* in more general terms, explaining that it is compositionally a lot more tightly constructed than it is usually considered to be, and identifying two compositional aspects that make this so. These two phenomena will be explained in the

---

[8]Steven E. Gilbert, *The Music of Gershwin* (New Haven and London: Yale University Press, 1995), 68-70. Reprinted by permission of Yale University Press.

chosen musical passage (discussed in the second paragraph): recursion (the passage begins and ends on the same chord, E7, while giving the impression of actually having gone somewhere) and transitionality (meaning that the passage serves as transition from mid-phrase to the next phrase, from cadenza material to the theme that immediately follows, and from rhythmic freedom to rhythmic stability). The reader is thus prepared for the detail immediately following. It then remains for the third paragraph to summarize the importance of the passage by explaining how a particular figure imbedded in the texture (E-D-C♯) relates to the harmony, and to connect the detail to the broader function of the passage.

These two analytical excerpts are very different in approach, yet each reaches its goal fairly quickly, with a minimum of jargon. One point illustrated here is that there is no single analytical template: there are many persuasive approaches to analysis. In addition to the harmonic, Schenkerian, and set-theory approaches, an analyst might address (for example) surface gestures, scansion and phraseology, or any of a number of stylistic features.

The analyst's business, explaining how a piece works, often consists of pointing out what is noteworthy or interesting about it—why this piece works differently from others. Because accounting for *everything* in a piece is both foolhardy and impossible, the analytical approach needs to be clearly established at the beginning of an analysis so that the reader has a clear idea of which questions are going to be asked of a piece. Once the frame of reference is clear, the analysis—of whatever length—can begin to unfold.

The best analyses tread between the subtle and the more apparent. As Jan LaRue put it: "Successful style analysis combines dissection with selection, insight with overview. If we mindlessly proliferate observed details, we may never reach larger understanding."[9] This is only one such balance: analysis also dances between the uniqueness of each artwork and its generic or stylistic relation to other works, between the obscure and what is readily apprehended, and between borrowing from different analytical systems or striking out on one's own. Analysis has the potential to be among the most rigorous and ultimately enlightening activities concerned with music study and musical writing.

---

[9]Jan LaRue, *Guidelines for Style Analysis* [1970], 2nd ed. (Warren, MI: Harmonie Park Press, 1992), 4.

4

Three Kinds of Practical Writing

*Even now do you think it's much fun for me to be tied to this
infernal galley-oar of journalism which affects every aspect of my
career? I am so ill that I can hardly hold my pen, yet I am forced to
write for my miserable hundred francs . . . [1]*

—HECTOR BERLIOZ

The writer on musical subjects will be called upon to produce a good deal
more than such traditional college assignments as research papers and
opinion essays. Several genres of practical writing are found in the musical world: genres that fulfill specific needs, address specific audiences,
and sometimes follow specific protocols. (One of these, the concert review, is discussed in Chapter 2.) Command of these kinds of writing enables one:

- to gain experience with the arts community in general, learning
  what is viable regarding both writing and musical performance
- to become acquainted with the members of the arts community,
  making friends and profitable connections

---

[1]Letter to his son Louis, 14 February 1861, in Humphrey Searle, ed. and
trans., *Hector Berlioz: A Selection from His Letters* (New York: Harcourt, Brace,
1966), 169.

- to advocate in effective writing for one's own musical efforts, persuasively communicating the musician's perspective to others who do not share or identify with that perspective
- (occasionally) to make some money

It would be misleading to suggest that there is substantially more money in writing about music than there is in playing or teaching it. As with any endeavor, though, increased experience and skill means that "no money" may become "some money," with further increases depending on skill and situation. The potential benefits of effective writing about music extend well beyond the classroom.

PROGRAM AND LINER NOTES

There are many approaches to writing program notes and liner notes (the printed commentaries that accompany recordings), and every approach is a compromise. Some readers are musically literate but most are probably not, some have performance experience and some do not, some know the repertoire intimately and some do not, and some are passionately devoted to the music being performed and others are not—at all. Given this spectrum, is it necessary that the annotator take everyone into account? Of course not. Must he or she try to reach the largest cross-section possible? Certainly.

For most readers, program notes that use complex technical vocabulary, feature notated musical examples, and detail formal processes are a wasted effort. Listeners who have a solid musical background can recognize themes and their musical adventures without having them notated, while those with less experience will be intimidated or put off by academic apparatus they do not understand. Likewise, play-by-play writing (as discussed in Chaper 3: "after a second statement in the tonic, a modulatory passage occurs; following the establishment of a new key, the secondary theme group then makes its appearance, opening with an upward-reaching figure that peaks on a high A before descending gently back to the C below . . .") helps little in appreciating or understanding a musical work—unless one plans to listen with a flashlight trained on both the score and the program notes. Program notes have often been written this way; who the authors expected to reach has never been clear.

A more destructive approach is one that trivializes the music under discussion. Although predicated on the belief that classical music is valuable, in an educational, high-culture, eat-your-spinach-because-it's-good-for-you sort of way, this approach targets an imaginary, ultimately disrespected "common person." Writing of this kind is likely to emphasize the prurient or sordid aspects of composers' biographies, to make forced attempts at humor, or to use slang and vernacular inappropriately. The net effect is to insult the reader and trivialize the music, thereby conveying the idea that, since the "entertainment" has to be provided in the commentary, the music must not be worth hearing. In general, program annotations are a poor venue for humor.

Humor in writing has a tendency to fall flat or, worse, to demean its subject. While a musical work may be hilarious, a joke explained is often a joke neutralized. Musical humor can certainly be identified, or a humorous plot explained quickly and deftly, but this is something very different from "laughing with" or "laughing at." Unless one seeks to be a musical humorist (the likes of Victor Borge, Anna Russell, and Peter Schickele—a.k.a. P.D.Q. Bach—are few), a frivolous posture on the part of the annotator does far more harm than good.

The advice so far has been negative. But these suggestions—that the author should seek to reach the broadest cross-section of the audience, that play-by-play and advanced vocabulary are unhelpful, that even *seeming* to trivialize the music is always wrong—are intended not as scolding but as signposts toward the fruitful directions that notes and commentary can take. Given a general audience ranging from musical novice to experienced listener, what kinds of information will prove to be both helpful and readily understood?

Biographical Background

Biographical information on the composer of a work, judiciously selected and treated, without undue stress on the composer's personal life, makes a good starting point. It can both situate a piece at a particular point in the composer's life (reckless youth? turbulent middle years? magisterial old age?), and connect the work of art with the aspects of being human we all share: living in the world and negotiating its difficulties, having or not having a family, earning recognition and a living, and maintaining a relationship with the wider world of one's peers. Biographical information can establish, for many listeners, a familiar resonance in a largely alien historical realm, thereby opening further doors into that realm.

Cultural Context

We often forget how remote a contemporary listener is from the cultural environment in which much concert music was produced. What did an eighteenth-century listener expect of a sonata, a symphony, an opera, or a sacred work? How do that listener's expectations differ from what we expect today? What aspects of the work in question would listeners have found surprising or astounding? For example, listeners today are so familiar with the technical fireworks of Liszt's piano music, which are now well within the capabilities of many conservatory students and university-level piano majors, that they do not realize that this music was all but unplayable for the vast majority of pianists throughout a good portion of Liszt's lifetime—and that his keyboard talents were therefore sometimes suspected of being supernatural. Finding a way to relate each piece to its own world helps the audience to see it as something other than a relic, and that is always more interesting to the listener than "Here is [yet] one more virtuosic piece by that master of the violin, Fritz Kreisler . . ."

Style and Affect

It is a good idea for the annotator to say a word or two about style and mood. A listener who knows a work will not be offended by an intelligent reminder of something already understood, and it will not hurt for another listener, one perhaps more familiar with such popular classical works as Pachelbel's D major canon and Tchaikovsky's suite from the *Nutcracker* ballet, to be made aware that the knotty dissonances of a Bartók string quartet are about to be heard, or that the ironic, painful emotional content of a Shostakovich symphony is about to be experienced. But finer points of musical style are best left alone, in consideration of the needs and experience of the average audience member. A good rule of thumb is for the commentary to provide, in addition to whatever biographical and historical context the annotator deems helpful, one or at most a very few things to listen for. More than this is probably too much.

One approach to organizing program notes is simple: treat each piece individually. In the following passage, student Dawn Kummer discusses J. S. Bach's second sonata for solo violin.

> J. S. Bach wrote his six pieces (three sonatas and three partitas) for solo violin over a six-year period that began in 1717. At this time, he was Kapellmeister and Director of Chamber Music for Prince Leopold of Anhalt-Cöthen. The Brandenburg concertos and his six 'cello suites also date from this period.

The movements of *Sonata no. 2 in A minor* follow the typical Baroque pattern of slow-fast-slow-fast. The first movement, marked *grave,* consists of a single melodic line, with double-, triple-, and quadruple-stops adding harmonic interest. It serves as a reflective introduction to the second movement, a fugue. Although it is not unusual to find Bach writing fugues, the violin seems ill-suited to carry more than one line at once. It is an amazing compositional feat that Bach could compose an entire fugue playable on the violin. This movement is entirely based on an eight-note theme which appears often in its original form and in inversion. The third movement of this sonata is marked *Andante* and contains two repeating sections. Its introspective melody floats over perpetual eighth-note accompaniment. The fourth and final movement, also in two repeated sections, is in lively contrast to the previous movement. Its running sixteenth and thirty-second notes bring the piece to a satisfying conclusion.

Ms. Kummer helps us view this piece from several angles. She provides a bit of historical background on the composer and his situation when he composed the piece, she includes a line about what might normally be expected in a similar piece from this time (that is, a Baroque sonata), and then she proceeds to a short discussion of each of the movements. These discussions are not overly technical, yet we see that her intended audience is probably a university community rather than the general public. For example, Ms. Kummer assumes that we know enough about the violin to understand that double-stops refers to the number of strings that are "stopped" by the left hand and bowed at the same time, and she finds no need to offer a definition of fugue, with its complex of key areas and entries, or to explain how fugues might be difficult to play on an instrument with only four strings. All this is obvious to trained musicians, but they are not a majority of the general public. No harm done—as long as the audience for whom the notes are intended is adequately prepared.

The problems attendant on writing for the general, symphony-attending public, though, are very different. On the one hand, it is dangerous to assume that the audience has any musical training at all; readers unfamiliar with the annotator's terms or concepts may feel insulted or alienated. On the other hand, any art music (including Western symphonic music) is an acquired taste, and those who are interested in it probably have a strong educational background and cultural awareness—and they will be put off by too chatty a tone or too simplistic a discussion. Thus the difficulty in writing for the general public lies in striking a balance between a high level of education and a merely rudimentary understanding of music.

One elegant solution to this problem is seen in the following discussion of Antonín Dvořák's *Carnival Overture* by Deborah Kauffman, who is program annotator for the Greeley Philharmonic Orchestra in Greeley, Colorado.

Antonín Dvořák (1841–1904) is certainly the most well-known composer of Czech origin, and also the most adept at melding Czech folk idioms and influences into Western orchestral music. Although he rarely quoted Czech folk music directly, Dvořák used its unique musical elements to create a distinctive folk sound in his own works. His melodic gifts were remarkable; the flowing melodies seem to spring forth effortlessly, supported by Dvořák's colorful, imaginative writing and clear formal structures.

Most of Dvořák's early musical training was on the violin and viola, although he also received instruction on the piano and organ at the Prague Organ School, where he studied the various skills required of a church organist and choir master. His music came to the attention of the public in 1877, when he entered the competition for the Austrian State Stipendum, an award established to support young, talented musicians. One of the judges was Johannes Brahms, who took it upon himself to recommend Dvořák's music to his own publisher, Simrock, who then commissioned Dvořák's first set of Slavonic Dances. Their popularity led to other commissions and performances, and Dvořák soon achieved widespread fame and recognition, traveling to conduct his own works across Europe.

Dvořák is also noteworthy for his support of Czechoslovakian nationalism at a time when the region was under the rule of the Austrian Habsburg empire. Dvořák wrote songs and operas in the Czech language, and struggled against anti-Czech feeling in Europe that often discouraged performance opportunities.

After a heated exchange with his publisher over Dvořák's insistence on the appearance of his musical titles in both German and Czech, Dvořák wrote:

> Your last letter, in which you launched forth into national-political explanations, amused me greatly; but I am sorry you are so badly informed. . . . But *what have we two to do with politics,* let us be glad that we can *dedicate our services solely to the beautiful art!* And let us hope that nations who represent and *possess art* will never perish, even though they may be small. Forgive me for this, but I just wanted to tell you that an artist too has a fatherland in which he must also have a firm faith and which he must love.

Dvořák also felt strongly about supporting the national music of other countries, particularly the United States, where he spent two years as the head of the National Conservatory in New York. He became fascinated with Native American Indian music and with the American Negro spiritual, the music he felt should be the basis for an American school of composition.

The *Carnival Overture* is the second of a triptych of overtures written by Dvořák in 1891 (the others are *In Nature's Realm* and *Othello*). It is dedicated to Cambridge University, which had bestowed an honorary doctoral degree upon the composer in June of that same year. The overture is generally programmatic, in that it portrays the sounds and feelings of a carnival scene, but does not try to portray any specific story. The boisterous outer sections have the feeling of a folk dance, while the slow middle section has a pastoral, outdoor mood, evoked by the haunting sound of the English horn and the shimmering strings.

Note that the treatment of the *Carnival Overture* itself is confined to the final paragraph, which summarizes the work's genesis, gives a general comment about approach (that the work is roughly descriptive), and offers a brief formal description of the work: three-part form, the central section's pastoral mood contrasting with the boisterous outer sections. This information provides more than enough for the untrained audience members to listen for: mood, compositional approach, general structure. But the bulk of the program annotation is an elegantly encapsulated life-and-times of the composer. We learn about his birth, his musical upbringing and development, Brahms's recognition and appreciation of his work, and his nationalist sympathies—his love for his own Czech heritage and his interest in ethnic musics of the New World. A nice added touch is the inclusion of the composer's own words, which set in relief a figure who is, after all, historically remote. The audience is informed, not insulted, and at the same time inordinate demands have not been made of its musical comprehension.

An audience's relative lack of experience with a particular musical style, practice, or environment is more an opportunity than a limitation for the annotator, who seeks to teach. One strategy that goes beyond individual treatments of the works to be heard will first address the concert program as a whole, discussing whatever stylistic, cultural, or historical background is common to the repertoire, and then go on to examine each work individually. This was the approach I took in producing a set of notes for a concert of popular Russian works: the overture to Glinka's *Russian i Liudmila*, Chaikovsky's second symphony, and Rachmaninov's *Rhapsody on a Theme of Paganini*. A general introduction to the Russian musical climate of the late nineteenth and early twentieth centuries is helpful for a concert audience, both as context for the works to be heard and because so many other Russian works remain in the concert repertoire.

Three Russian Romantics
Jonathan Bellman

Few nineteenth-century musical styles captivated Europe as did that of the emergent Russian Romantic School. Because it was profoundly personal and nationalistic, Russian music had strongly exotic connotations for musicians and audiences further west who were largely unfamiliar with it. The various contributions of the multifaceted Russian musical community, which included Chaikovsky's conservatory training and polish, Balakirev's broad sweep and rough edges, Cui's influential role as figurehead and advocate, and (later) the supreme instrumental virtuosity and musical assurance of Rachmaninov, still somehow had enough in common for an instantly recognizable Russian "sound" and personality to characterize many of the works of this era. This was a sound so compelling that it sent composers of other peripheral European countries scurrying to uncover and utilize musical diamonds from their own countries and cultures.

Mikhail Ivanovich Glinka (1804-1857)
Overture to *Ruslan i Liudmila* (1842)

Glinka, as a result of his unsystematic musical training and directionless (although promising) youth, may seem an unlikely candidate to found a school of Russian composition. His opera *A Life for the Tsar* (1836) did accomplish this: its patriotic plot and musically nationalistic overtones enjoyed a huge success with both nobility and populace. By contrast, *Ruslan i Liudmila*, his second opera, is more exotic than nationalistic in tone. The plot is based on a poem of Alexander Pushkin, a fantasy about the princess Liudmila, her imprisonment by an evil dwarf named Chernomor, and her rescue by and marriage to Ruslan, the hero.

The overture is both a virtuoso showpiece and a staple of the orchestral repertoire. A vigorous opening of bright, brassy chords and swirling strings sets the tone, and the listener is immediately treated to a shimmering, kaleidoscopically changing texture composed of alternating and overlapping instrumental groups. As the work unfolds, "eastern" musical coloring is used to suggest the Tartar prince Ratmir and the Varangian chieftain Farlaf, both of whom will seek Liudmila's hand. Finally, Chernomor makes his musical appearance at the end with a descending whole-tone scale, lending an even more exotic character to the musical language of this colorful work.

Peter Ilyich Chaikovsky (1840-1893)
Symphony no. 2, the "Little Russian" (1872, revised 1880)

Chaikovsky's superb craftsmanship, the result of disciplined conservatory study, was both envied and mistrusted by rougher-hewn nationalists like Balakirev, who recognized his talent but criticized his perceived Western orientation. The occasional musical excesses often attributed to Chaikovsky's troubled emotional life are nowhere to be found here; instead, the second symphony, written during his most nationalistic period, is a tightly organized and compelling work based primarily on themes from the Ukraine (an area known as "Little Russia").

The first movement begins with a slow introduction based on one of these Ukrainian folk tunes. Here Chaikovsky uses a

variation technique that originated with Glinka: at each thematic
repetition, the background and texture is varied in some way
while the theme remains relatively unchanged. The basis of the
second movement is a bridal march Chaikovsky wrote for an
early opera; the same Russian variation technique is used with
the main theme, which is also of Ukrainian origin. The scherzo
movement is in a brisk triple meter, but it shifts to duple for a
contrasting middle section. The finale, based on the folk song
"The Crane," is so completely Russian as to sound almost like
Mussorgsky. Or perhaps the similarity runs the opposite way:
Mussorgsky's "Promenade" from *Pictures at an Exhibition*
(1874; written two years after Chaikovsky completed his first
version of this symphony) bears a striking resemblance to the
grand opening statement of the theme of Chaikovsky's finale.
Later in the movement, Chaikovsky uses a whole-tone scale and
a jagged bass figure as background, opting for strikingly "Russian" textures over more traditional consonant accompaniments.
The climax suggests, with its wild joy and hint of suppressed
fury, the abandon of a Cossack dance.

Sergei Rachmaninov (1873-1943)
Rhapsody on a Theme of Paganini, op. 43 (1934).

The *Rhapsody on a Theme of Paganini*, a series of variations upon the violinist Niccolò Paganini's famous 24th Caprice,
exemplifies another staple of the Russian musical style: extro-
verted virtuoso pianism. Rachmaninov's fame rests equally
upon his dual careers as concert pianist and composer, so it is
not surprising that his piano works have proven to be his most
famous. This work is a favorite of pianists and audiences alike,
and it uses a wide variety of pianistic fireworks in the service of
a concise and witty structure. The seventh variation includes a
fascinating touch; by quoting the chant melody *Dies Irae* (from
the Catholic Mass for the Dead) Rachmaninov pays tribute to a
famous variation set for piano and orchestra by another pianist-
composer, the *Totentanz* of Franz Liszt, which uses the *Dies
Irae* as its primary theme. Perhaps the most famous variation in
the *Rhapsody* is the thirteenth; this D-flat major reverie (distant indeed from the A minor tonic) is based on the inversion of
the theme—that is, Rachmaninov simply turns his melody up-

side down. What follows is the sprint to the finish line: a Lisztian hail of scales, chords, and octaves brings the piece to a blazing conclusion.

My goal in these notes was to tie the experience of many listeners—that many Russian works somehow "sound Russian" even when they do not sound like each other—to three very different musical works. With this in mind, I used the opening section to introduce the Russian sound in general and to outline several musical styles and personalities that have contributed to the Russian repertory. In the sections dealing with individual works, ideas already stated (such as Rachmaninov's instrumental command) are briefly reiterated as preparation for hearing a specific piece of music and understanding key elements. In the case of the Rachmaninov *Rhapsody,* I wanted to stress the work's many points of intersection with other virtuoso piano repertoire.

The annotator walks several thin lines. They lie between what the listener probably already knows and what may be entirely new; between what is musically obvious and what may require more listener concentration to pick up; and—most difficult of all—between the inappropriate extreme (what is either simple-minded or hopelessly obscure) on the one hand and that golden area of new material or concepts that listeners are prepared to learn on the other. Each audience presents a different challenge, as does each new concert program.

Finally, don't analyze! Analysis is rarely of use to the concertgoer. A memorably damning statement about program-note analyses was offered by Claude Debussy's colleague in music criticism, the French writer Colette. After a performance of a symphony for which the composer provided a thematic analysis in notes that were distributed to the audience, Colette wrote:

> But then the program did its best to explain. . . . How obliging of it! It said, for example, "The rhythmic transformations of figures 4 and 5 lead theme 1 through progressively increasing note values." . . . Then a restatement of the introduction, reexposition, etc. There are, perhaps, people for whom such artifice aids comprehension; it merely makes me feel a fool.[2]

----

[2]As quoted in Claude Debussy, *Debussy on Music,* col. and int. by François Lesure, trans. and ed. by Richard Langham Smith (New York: Alfred A. Knopf, 1977), 128.

It was a gross misjudgment on the composer's part to assume that a detailed look into his compositional workshop would enhance the enjoyment of the audience at large. Composers do not, as a rule, produce artworks only for the delectation of specialists; far more often they seek to communicate with a broad cross-section of humanity. For the program annotator or the composer to provide an analysis for the first-time listener seems to be a sure way for this kind of direct communication *not* to happen.

SUMMARIES AND ABSTRACTS

Summaries and abstracts represent two different solutions to a frequently misunderstood problem. The problem lies in rendering in a few words (exactly how few will vary with the situation) the essence of a large piece of writing such as a scholarly article, a master's thesis, or a doctoral dissertation. Since the entire content cannot be retained, decisions regarding what to include and omit must be made at the beginning. The preference for either summary or abstract will depend on the use for which it is intended.

The Summary

A formal *summary* explains what the author was doing in a particular piece of writing and what results were shown or conclusions drawn. Summaries emphasize that the article in question is being described by a third party, so constructions like "the author states" and "this study shows" may occasionally be used. (While some writers forbid the use of such phrases, I consider it permissible. The emphasis or de-emphasis of the author's role is one of the key differences between summaries and abstracts; summaries *stress* the author's role and responsibility, and abstracts do not.) Another element specific to summaries is that more weight is placed on the conclusions: what was shown, what came to be proven, what resulted. Summaries are often used in annotated bibliographies and the literature review sections of theses and dissertations, two kinds of writing in which a variety of sources are examined and evaluated, so the emphasis on results and conclusions is appropriate.

Here is an example of an article summary, written by student Amie Margoles. The article is "No Movie Without Music" by Verle Ormsby, Jr., which appeared in *Director Plus* (1:4, 1994). This publication, which calls itself "a music education forum from United Musical Instruments U.S.A, Inc.," functions both as a magazine intended for instrumental teachers and conductors and as publicity and advertising material for United Musical Instruments.

> In this article, Dr. Ormsby describes how six "first call" French horn players in the Hollywood film industry are among the most widely heard musicians world-wide. According to Ormsby, horn parts are prominent in the scores of most of Hollywood's blockbuster films. These films are viewed and heard by millions of people throughout the world. These musicians have arisen from dozens of talented professional horn players who have sought to get into Hollywood studio work. Ormsby asserts that the long hours and demands of recording, strong competition, and extreme variance of scores and direction have weeded out all but the hardiest, most consistent, and most talented horn players. As a result, he believes, this elite handful of players have developed French horn playing for films into a refined, high-quality, and demanding art form.

The primary focus here is the conclusion: how superior the top studio horn players are and how often they are heard worldwide. Other information follows from that: the competition they faced, the skills they have to master, and how they have shaped the art form in which they work. This summary would be appropriate for use in an annotated bibliography; the reader would get a clear idea of both the main point of the article and the related issues the author addresses.

The Abstract

A formal *abstract* is a purely academic kind of writing, a presentation of the article itself in miniature, and it is proportionally similar to the original: introduction, premises, evidence, discussion, conclusions. Unlike summaries, abstracts place more emphasis on methodology, argument, and proof—that is, not just the conclusions, but rather how the author arrives at them. In scholarly publications, abstracts often accompany the articles upon which they are based, and they also appear in collections and standard bibliographic databases (such as *RILM Abstracts of Musical Literature*).

A good abstract enables a reader—perhaps a student or scholar who needs to be aware of developments in a particular field but does not have the leisure to read every article in detail—to get a clear idea of not only what an article concludes but what the author's methodology was and what evidence was marshalled in support of the conclusions. The reader finds more information in a strong abstract than in a summary because it addresses not only the destination but the nature of the journey, the steps taken to arrive at the conclusions.

Another important difference between abstracts and summaries is that summaries stress the role of the author in the writing (Ms. Margoles uses the phrases "Dr. Ormsby describes" and "Ormsby asserts"). Abstracts, however, should be written from (so to speak) inside the article. The person producing the abstract acts as author of the article (and articles are often abstracted by their authors): stating the problem, presenting evidence, pointing to the conclusions—all in a very few words—without suggesting that another piece of writing is being discussed.

Here is Ms. Margoles's abstract of the same article on studio horn players:

> Alfred Brain and Vince De Rosa were for a long time the pre-eminent French horn players in film studio music. These musicians rose from a host of exceptional pre-war players including Wendell Hoss (Disney), Jack Carol (MGM), Jimmy Stagliano (Fox), and George Hoffman (Warner Brothers). Brain established a high standard of musicianship and De Rosa introduced the Conn 8D as a solution to the intonation problems of the European horns, once favored in studio music. The large-bore Conn 8D handled the lower ranges of modern horn solos and had an easily adjustable pitch, needed to blend with many groups of instruments. Since the late 1940s, De Rosa has played in every major Hollywood film, often recording three to five films a week. Competition for such exposure is extreme and, at present, the field of active "first call"

players has dropped from about fifty to six, including the still-active
De Rosa and five of his former students.

She begins where the article does, by introducing two of the main
characters in her story (that is, Dr. Ormsby's story, but for the purposes
of the abstract it is hers). She talks about some of their colleagues, then
gives a short explanation of what each of the two individuals contributed:
musicianship in one case, the particular choice of horn in the other—
which itself needs a short explanation. She then outlines the diabolical
schedule of a first-call horn player and offers a neat conclusion: not only
is one individual still productive after decades of this work, but the other
first-call horn players are all his former students. While virtually the entire summary dealt with six first-call players, in the abstract they appear
only in the final sentence—but we have a much better idea of their place
in the broader studio horn scene: the environment from which they
emerged, the challenges they regularly face, and the relevance of their
chosen instrument to their success.

Summaries and abstracts are thus two discrete but often confused
forms. Unfortunately, what are in fact summaries are often mislabeled
abstracts (the opposite mistake is not made nearly as often). But writing
them is an extremely valuable exercise: reducing another author's article
to a miniature requires a familiarity and understanding of the original article or work that even two or three close readings will not yield. For an
article central to your field, an article you absolutely have to know, the
abstracting process is invaluable.

THE PRESS RELEASE

The press release, properly done, demands as little creativity as possible.
(I distinguish between actual press releases and press announcements
that inflate themselves by inappropriately incorporating advertising copy
and puff material. There is no need to discuss the latter variety, which is
writing intended to mislead.) The function of a press release is to publi-
cize an upcoming event, and you want it to be as effective as possible.
The difficulty lies in the fact that press releases can be used in different
ways. A press release provides basic information that can be presented in
various formats: as published listings of events, as announcements and
fliers, or as a Public Service Announcement to be read aloud on a local

radio station. For such uses, only basic information is appropriate: who, what, when, where, how much. In as concise a fashion as possible, people need to be told who is playing the concert, what kind of concert it is, when and where people should show up for it, how much money they will need for tickets, and how they can get further information. Traditionally, the last two items, ticket prices and an information number, close the press release.

This is all the hard information that is necessary. But because newspapers sometimes print press releases verbatim as mini-articles, more is required when writing one. Since space is of paramount concern in newspaper writing, the author of a press release must use what is called "pyramid form," where the absolutely essential material occurs at the beginning, and what follows is helpful but less and less necessary. (The name derives from the idea that chunks of the press release may have to be deleted, and this form makes the editing process unproblematic—when the bottom chunk is cut off, the "pyramid" still stands; it is simply smaller.) Here is an example, written by Susan Nelson, the Director of Arts Information at the University of Northern Colorado:

November 19, 1993

FOR MORE INFORMATION CONTACT:

Susan Nelson, 123-4567

The University of Northern Colorado's Concert Band,

Symphonic Band, and Wind Ensemble will perform at 8 p.m. on

Tuesday, November 23, at Foundation Hall, 1516 Eighth Avenue.

Under the direction of Dr. Kenneth Singleton and Dr. Richard

Mayne, the ensembles will present a wide variety of band

literature. The UNC bands have received national and international

recognition, with ensembles having been invited to perform at

numerous state and national conventions, and having produced a

series of important wind recordings and publications.

The performance is open to the public without charge. For

more information, please contact the UNC Bands Office at 345-6789.

The final two sentences about cost and contact information are *not* optional; in this example the base of the pyramid must remain. In the computer age, deleting a block from the middle of a press release is no more complex than cutting off the end. But note the general adherence to a pyramid approach: what is most important about the event is stated in the first brief paragraph. For the newspaper, and for others that might need more and want to quote directly, the names of the directors and comments on the repertoire and the reputation of the bands (all on an appropriate, publicity-based level) are provided.

Another possibility is to include in the release quotations from a participant and to provide more information. In the following four-paragraph example, the structure is a true pyramid: each paragraph is of slightly less importance, and the release could function in one-, two-, or three-paragraph versions. Information may easily be gleaned from it for radio announcements, and the whole still works fine as a newspaper article.

Nov. 20, 1990

FOR FURTHER INFORMATION CONTACT:

Susan Nelson, 123-4567

An evening of dance will be presented by the University of Northern Colorado Dance Department at 7:30 p.m. Tuesday, Dec. 4, in Gunter Hall, room 107, 10th Avenue and Cranford Place, Greeley.

An informal showcase, the Gunter Hall performances will feature the department's Dance Tour Troupe and several of the dance classes. Tickets cost $2 apiece, with proceeds to benefit the UNC Dance Scholarship Fund. For tickets and additional information, call the dance department, 234-5678.

"The evening is presented as an opportunity for members of the Beginning Jazz and Modern Dance, as well as the Intermediate Jazz, Ballet, and Modern Dance classes, to show off what they've learned," said Carolyn Genoff Campbell, head of the Dance Tour Troupe. "It's a way for class members to perform for roommates, friends and parents, and apply what they've learned to a performance situation."

> The evening will also include a performance by the department's Dance Tour Troupe, 12 students who choreograph their own works under the supervision of [the Director] and perform at schools throughout Colorado. Formed in 1977, the troupe presents a variety of dance styles, including Jazz, modern, lyrical, and primitive, to audiences of all ages.

The central idea with press releases, abstracts, summaries, and other kinds of "occasional" writing such as publicity puff pieces is that the author's personality, mastery of the language, and unique voice *need to be well in the background.* (This is less true for program or liner notes.) Practical writing has specific purposes, and it must satisfy these purposes in order to provide readers what they need. There is little romance here! But compare this kind of writing with other musical activity. The greatest musical virtuosi, the interpreters with the most profound command of their instruments, have spent long hours practicing technical exercises. Similarly, the greatest composers, historically, spent much of their training not only copying over other composers' works but producing highly structured and formulaic exercises in counterpoint and harmony. So it is with all kinds of practical writing: the discipline is irreplaceable, much experience may be gained, and a good deal about craftsmanship may be learned from such clearly defined tasks.

5

Opinion and the Writing of an Effective Essay

There is nothing more difficult than talking about music.[1]

—CAMILLE SAINT-SAËNS

Producing an essay that persuades someone to your way of thinking, or at least raises doubts in the mind of a reader holding the opposite position, is a consummate challenge. As with other genres, the author has to strike balances: between an inflammatory tone and an inoffensively bland one, between unsupported raving and an argument smothered in supporting data. Command of the essay form, once achieved, will benefit every other genre of writing; research papers, reviews, and program notes are shaped by a writer's persuasiveness in the same way that essays invariably benefit from the author's command of research method, listening skills, and quality of musical understanding. So, although essays on musical subjects are far more common inside the university environment than outside it, the skills learned in essay preparation will benefit a lifetime of writing. As the practical musician isolates a technical or interpretive problem to solve through focused effort, so the author seeks to master persuasion by writing essays.

---

[1]As quoted in James Harding, *Saint-Saëns and His Circle* (London: Chapman & Hall, 1965), v.

69

PRESENTATION AND TONE

Organization

In an essay, as with concert reviews and program notes (discussed in Chapters 2 and 4), decisions regarding organization need to be made before the writing begins. This does *not* mean that these decisions, once made, are irrevocable; rather, it means that arguments are best laid out within a broader framework. The framework may well be changed later, and such a change will likely necessitate adjustments in the writing. But proceeding toward completion with the guidance of a well-considered outline (more on outlines below) is far more effective than beginning to write with a blank screen or a blank piece of paper. Since the central goal of an essay is persuasion, there is much more for the author to consider than mere evidence or the intrinsic merit of the position to be defended. Organization and presentation require care.

Thoughts must proceed in a logical sequence; transitions must be clear, convincing, and *not* jarring; and conclusions must follow naturally, as the obvious and unavoidable results of the ideas presented. It is especially important to follow this formula when your point is speculative or controversial. The more radical the idea, the more ironclad the presentation must be, since the resistance it must overcome will be greater.

Confrontational Writing

Writers, professionals as well as undergraduates, often assume that a confrontational approach results in vigorous, persuasive writing. Confrontational writing implies, by its very nature, that if an idea is worth holding, all other ideas ought to be disparaged, even with hostility and resentment. Politically influenced writing sometimes inspires this kind of excess; authors flatter themselves in believing that stakes are much higher than with "mere" academic or musical issues. Locating one's musical or critical position within Inexorable Historical Forces or the Great Moral Balance lends, not surprisingly, a sense of self-righteousness and desperation to the discussion. In all cases, we must remember that however firmly we hold a position, we seek to inform and persuade, not harangue and incite.

Because confrontational writing is both uncivil and counterproductive, it is wrong, as the following examples will illustrate. Since it is not limited to writing influenced by political thought, I deliberately avoid using politically influenced examples so as to leave questions of ideological loyalties out of the discussion altogether. Consider, instead, this final portion of the final paragraph of Harold Truscott's scholarly introduction to an edition of the piano sonatas of Johann Nepomuk Hummel (1778-1837), a slightly younger contemporary of Beethoven and a student of Mozart and Muzio Clementi. The balance of the introduction has addressed Hummel's biography, his musical compositions, and matters of style, interpretation, and performance practices relevant to the study of his music. Until its final section it is completely appropriate, a helpful guide to the music it introduces. In closing, Truscott suggests that the best technical preparation for studying Hummel's sonatas may be the exercises in Clementi's *Gradus ad Parnassum*. He then (inexplicably) concludes:

> By the time this work [*Gradus*] has been mastered, the pianist will be ready to tackle any type of piano technique, excluding those techniques (if that is the word) known as avant-garde. For plucking piano strings, sawing off piano legs or in other ways destroying the instrument, sitting in silence watching the piano warily in case it bites, and hitting the keyboard or producing *glissandi* with one's knuckles, forearms, nose or teeth, with the further aid of French chalk—or using what is called a "prepared" piano, which means that it is prepared for use as anything but a musical instrument—for these things Clementi did not provide. Grimaldi, or Grock, or some other such artist, I should say[,] would have been best equipped to produce a text-book or "method" on such matters. But Hummel's sonatas do not require these techniques. In addition to the physical techniques covered by Clementi's *Gradus*, they do require something else also covered by the Clementi work, but absent from the territory of avant-garde techniques, and that is musicianship.[2]

Mr. Truscott is welcome to his opinion about prepared pianos, nontraditional ways of playing traditional instruments (more accurately called "extended techniques"), John Cage's 4'33" (though it remains unnamed, there is a specific dig about this piece), and anything else. Nonetheless, he is not welcome to rant, and his inclusion of such a snide, off-topic closing section in a discussion of Hummel's piano sonatas goes well beyond authorial right and propriety. This passage may first strike readers as amusing, particularly if we are resistant to most piano music of the twentieth century (a position that may well change with more experience), but

[2]Harold Truscott, Foreword to Johann Nepomuk Hummel, *Complete Piano Sonatas* (London: Musica Rara, 1974), ix. Reprinted by permission of Musica Rara.

on sober reflection we wonder why the passage is there and why we are being confronted with a completely irrelevant matter.

Worse yet is the opening of Henry Pleasants's 1955 screed, *The Agony of Modern Music:*

> Serious Music is a dead art.
>
> The vein which for three hundred years offered a seemingly inexhaustible yield of beautiful music has run out. What we know as modern music is the noise made by deluded spectators picking through the slagpile.[3]

This passage is consciously insulting. It serves notice that the book will consist of variations on the Golden Age Fallacy: everything is terrible in these decadent times, and it was all much better before (whenever "before" might have been). The rhetoric, moreover, is dishonest: Pleasants's aesthetic contrast, "beautiful" music with "the noise made by deluded spectators," masks the implied moral contrast: seriousness vs. the slagpile, value vs. accumulated waste. His tone is indefensible, and for an attentive reader it undermines his position through its very shrillness. When an author yells or sneers rather than presents an idea for consideration with at least a modicum of civility, when a statement seems more suited to a bumper sticker than a paper, article, or book, then it badly needs to be revised or thrown out.

I do not mean to imply that there is no merit in passionately held positions *per se,* political or otherwise, or that positions are not worth defending with conviction. Positions are, ideally, the products of our opinions, beliefs, and ultimately our values, and a well-reasoned and firmly held position says a great deal about the person holding it. But strength of position or belief is not the same thing as stridency of rhetoric. Writing that reflects solid convictions and clear thinking throughout, carefully crafted writing in which clear attention has been devoted to presentation, elegance, and rhetorical restraint, will always be more powerful and persuasive than such undisciplined venting as the Pleasants excerpt.

Stylistic Excess

Stylistic excess consists of attempts to fortify an argument (in the same way that breakfast cereals of arguable nutritional value are fortified with

---

[3]Henry Pleasants, *The Agony of Modern Music* (New York: Simon and Schuster, 1955), 3.

added vitamins and nutrients) with superlatives, overly colorful adjectives, or exaggerated wording. Compare the following two passages:

> M. Chopin is . . . a dealer in the most absurd and hyperbolical extravagances. . . . The entire works of Chopin present a motley surface of ranting hyperbole and excruciating cacophony. . . . There is an excuse at present for Chopin's delinquencies: he is entrammelled in the enthralling bonds of that arch-enchantress, George Sand, celebrated equally for the number and excellence of her romances and her lovers.[4]

> The music of Frédéric Chopin has shown a troubling predisposition for overstatement and dissonance, characteristics also seen in the writing of George Sand, with whom Chopin has shared his life for some years.

The difference in content is minimal; I drafted the second passage in an attempt to reword the first as calmly as possible. Writing such as the former amounts to overkill, an assemblage of highly charged, multisyllabic words that dulls the reader's senses. Note, too, the first statement's confrontational undercurrent: to oppose the author's evaluation would be to stand up and defend "ranting hyperbole and excruciating cacophony." This kind of disrespect is troubling and unnecessary. While lunacies meriting wording this strong may (with some effort) be imagined, in almost all cases such excesses are unwarranted. Writing of this kind proclaims, paradoxically, that the argument itself is too weak to stand on its own.

THE WRITING PROCESS: FROM OUTLINE TO FINAL DRAFT

Essay writing, as stated above, needs to take place within the framework of a plan. This plan, the outline, is a requirement for virtually all writing, and arranging the parts of the outline in the most effective order is not a job to be rushed. A good outline facilitates prose writing in all ways: it insures that a project is logically thought through at the outset, it provides the structural roadmap by which the writing can proceed, and it will ultimately prove to be a lifeline to authors who get lost in their own prose, arguments, subject matter, or voluminous notes. (This includes all of us,

---

[4]Anonymous review in the *Musical World* (London), 28 October 1841, quoted in Nicholas Slonimsky, *Lexicon of Musical Invective* [1953] (London and Seattle: University of Washington Press, 1978), 84.

at one time or another.) Of course, outlines are not carved in stone; if the writing process comes to suggest a better way of organizing the paper, both outline and paper may be changed. But a well-considered and carefully crafted outline is the surest guide to a successfully organized and workable first draft, and it will ultimately save a great deal of work.

Let us examine a short essay by Jessica Mosier, an undergraduate cello student, and use it to illustrate the outlining process. She presents a defense of the Suzuki method of instrumental music pedagogy, based on her personal experience as a Suzuki piano and cello pupil. (Remember, our business is to examine this essay's organization and style; its appearance here is neither an endorsement of one method of instrumental instruction nor an implicit critique of any other method.)

The Suzuki method of learning to play an instrument is surrounded by controversy. Some people say that it is not a good way to learn to play an instrument. I disagree; I began learning the Suzuki method of piano at age six, and it was one of the best experiences I ever had. It taught me skills that I use today, not only in playing music, but also in other areas of my life.

One of these skills is the ability to listen. Along with the required Suzuki books, I was required to purchase tapes of the music being played. I listened to these tapes at every opportunity. Consequently, I knew the notes to the pieces before I even began to play them on the piano. After I knew the notes, it was just a matter of learning where to put my fingers. Even now, I listen to recordings of my repertoire before I begin playing it. I believe this gives me a head start in learning a piece because I know what it is supposed to sound like. This ability to listen also helps me today, because I have noticed that I pay closer attention in class than my peers who perhaps did not learn the Suzuki method. Even as a young child, I was trained to stop what I was doing and listen to the teacher giving directions. I feel that this training has helped me achieve higher grades because I always knew what was going on.

Another benefit of the Suzuki method is the belief that the parent is an important part of teaching the child. I began playing Suzuki cello at age nine, and my mother sat in on my lessons and took notes, just as she did when I took Suzuki piano. When it was time to practice at home, she was there with me to be sure that I practiced correctly. Since she had been at the lessons, she knew what to reinforce, and what to improve. She was also there to give me encouragement when I needed it most. I believe that this portion of the Suzuki method greatly promotes a nurturing family environment, which is something that is seriously lacking in our society today.

Still another skill I learned from the Suzuki method is the ability to concentrate. I believe that concentration is extremely important, not only in music, but also in other areas. When I practice in the university practice rooms, I find that I am able to tune out peripheral noise, and concentrate on my playing. Deep concentration such as this comes in very handy when I play recitals; I am able to forget that anyone else is in the room, aside from my accompanist. This ability to concentrate also helps me greatly when I take tests. I can tune out the noise of other people, and think only about the task at hand. As a result, I am not distracted by others' moving around while I am still taking the test.

Overall, I think that the Suzuki method is a very good way to learn an instrument because students learn not only music, but also skills that they will carry with them their whole lives.

Ms. Mosier's essay illustrates several effective strategies for persuasive writing. Her organization is clear: the opening paragraph explains the issue she intends to discuss, each of the next three paragraphs provides one supporting argument plus commentary and discussion, and the last paragraph is a single summarizing sentence. This organization, which reflects forethought, is the direct result of the outlining process. We can imagine that her first scrawled, brainstormed outline (or simple list of ideas) might have looked something like this:

Suzuki Method

1. Suzuki method--how it worked for me

2. Listening skills

3. Mom's role

4. Learning to concentrate

5. Conclusions

A rereading of this list suggests that while it is helpful, one cannot very well start writing from something so general. Accordingly, we can further imagine Ms. Mosier sitting down with her list and producing a second, fleshed-out version of the outline that could have looked something like the following.

I. Premise: Suzuki method as effective method of instrumental instruction

    A. Controversy about it

    B. List of objections

    C. My experience

    D. Other life skills taught

II. Listening skills

    A. Required tapes

        1. Knowing tunes before learning to play or read

        2. Repetition and Reinforcement

    B. Benefits in learning repertoire today--hearing it first

    C. Benefits in class, listening to teachers, higher grades, etc.

III. Mom's role

    A. Sat in on lessons, as per method, like a second teacher

        1. Could help me practice, reinforce corrections and work on areas needing improvement

        2. Could offer encouragement and support when needed--all week, not just at lesson

    B. Strengthens parent-child bond in general--much needed in
       families today, etc.

IV. Ability to concentrate

    A. Musical advantages

       1. Tuning out outside noise in practice rooms

       2. Concentrating during performance, not getting thrown by
          extraneous noise or movement

    B. Other advantages

       1. Test-taking--others' restlessness not bothering me

V. Conclusions (Whatever!)

From this outline, she could certainly begin to write, crafting a sentence or two for each idea, with the outline functioning as scaffolding. The result is a solid organizational structure, with clear, logical progress from initial idea to conclusions.

Notice also the advantage of using the writing process to reconsider each point in the outline, allowing for the possibility of changing one's mind. For example, item I.B, the list of others' objections to the method advocated, did not make it from the outline into the essay. Why, after all, list counterarguments? It is better to acknowledge, briefly, the objections but not to place specific doubts in readers' minds by listing them, even if one could respond to each. This approach represents an offensive rather than a defensive strategy, a more vigorous approach to persuasion than trying to foresee difficulties and disarm objections in advance.

One effective tactic was to link the musical advantages of the method to benefits enjoyed in nonmusical life. A paper aimed at musicians (or a music professor) thus connects its issues to the wider world and shows how a method of musical instruction also maximizes nonmusical skills. Listening and concentration skills in all areas are developed, the parent becomes a second Suzuki teacher, and the commitment of family members to each other is reinforced. (Ms. Mosier assumes that the reader will agree that this is a good thing, and for the majority of readers this is a safe assumption.) In this way the author strengthens her musical point by relating it to a far bigger picture. Since nonmusical benefits make up a good part of the Suzuki philosophy and tradition, this might seem (to those familiar with the Suzuki method) a relatively obvious card to play, but one aspect of good essay writing consists of perceiving such opportunities and capitalizing on them, placing one's material and reasoning in the most advantageous light.

To improve the essay further, the author might have expanded on her conclusions a little. She could have linked the method's initial approach to learning music—by ear rather than through reading—to the way children learn language, which is a centerpiece of the Suzuki philosophy. She could have pointed out that teaching life-skills (which she has discussed and applauded) and developing good citizens were greater priorities for Dr. Suzuki than training professional musicians. Unquestionably, she began too many sentences with "I," and phrases such as "some people say" (in the second sentence) are a bit too informal. But few essays, even published essays, are considered unimprovable by their authors, and in its current form this one illustrates much about persuasive writing and organization.

The idea that improvement is always possible, and always to be striven after, underlies a central point regarding revision: two drafts, a first and a final, even if the professor has annotated the first draft with suggestions for improvement, are not enough. Awkward passages and illogical changes of direction can be confusing to readers yet almost invisible to authors because the logic is their own—and they often need more than two drafts to find a problem. It is therefore advisable to outline the essay draft you consider to be final *after* it is written. This outline will demonstrate where transitions need to be used to guide the reader through the author's reasoning: *moreover, in contrast to, nonetheless, therefore,* and so on. In such an outline the building blocks of the essay will be apparent, and the author will then be able to use transitions to fashion a smooth and lucid paper, a real final draft.

HINTS ON BEGINNING

Almost all writers, student and professional, feel that beginning is especially difficult. One philosophy holds that one should begin by setting *anything* down on paper or computer screen, reasoning that it can always be changed. For this reason, one should not be too critical about the opening of a first draft. But some advance consideration will help insure that you make a strong beginning and move in the right direction. Acknowledging that even the most experienced authors sometimes find themselves stymied by an inability to begin (despite having much to say), here are some strategies to use when the author-to-be finds that the pump, so to speak, needs to be primed.

Ask yourself questions. What is my main point? How do I set it up, or lay out the data or arguments leading to it? How does the musical work I am discussing compare to other works of the same genre/from the same era/on the same concert? When a live performance is being discussed, how am I different from the way I was when I entered the hall? Why, in short, am I writing this? ("Because the silly thing is assigned," true or not, will not get you out of the starting blocks.)

If the opening is proving to be a major hurdle, don't begin with the opening sentence or paragraph. It is typical for the first five versions of an opening paragraph to be discarded. Why allow a difficulty with the opening to prevent you from making any progress whatsoever? Start with the second paragraph, or the second sentence, or anything you feel confident writing about *right now.* Perhaps this is background, or analyis, or even conclusions; regardless, begin writing at any point in the outline. The holes can be filled in later.

In the initial stages, do not be too self-critical. It is best for an author to complete a draft, one that covers the basic content from first to last, and then to start the revising process. Being compulsive about revising and correcting an opening paragraph or section as soon as it is written is less advisable; the subsequent lack of attention to other parts of the paper will show in the final product. Keep writing until you have a whole to work with, even if it is initially somewhat sloppy and misshapen.

COLLEGIAL EDITING: ESSAYS AS PEER REVIEW EXERCISES

Because of their relatively short length and emphasis on argument and persuasion, essays provide an ideal vehicle for an in-class peer-review exercise. Peer review has several advantages, not least among them being the fresh, critical evaluation by colleagues, readers other than the professor, readers who have not been laboring over each word as has the author. Not only authors benefit from this process; the editing experience to be gained by readers who are looking over unfamiliar papers with an eye toward sharpening and improving them will prove valuable in editing both their own and others' work. The process is analogous to that of a pre-recital coaching by someone other than one's teacher: a fresh pair of ears often yields fresh insights and perspectives, thereby enabling the performer to better focus an intepretation and performance.

A common way of facilitating this review process is to provide reviewers with a list of specific questions to be answered for every essay to be evaluated. Such questions, formulated to help focus the reviewers' thoughts, might address the overall point of each piece, whether each paragraph has a discernable point and whether it follows from the previous paragraph, which sentences need to be deleted, whether more transitions are necessary, and so on. Authors may then be presented with the readers' sheets and use them as guides to improve their essays.

Another method is for readers to note suggestions, objections, and questions in the margins of each paper and then use these annotations to guide the discussions. In my experience, more than enough suggestions for improvement result, and authors can jot down the suggestions on their own drafts in ways most comprehensible to them. The annotated draft approach also removes the additional step of a separate review sheet and the worry about specific questions on the sheet that it may not be helpful to address. Editing in the real world is done both ways.

Here is one paradigm for a peer review exercise.

1. The essay assignment is given, and the class is divided into groups of four. Students are instructed that their first submission draft should be accompanied by three photocopies for the other members of their group.

2. On the due date, the photocopies are distributed to the other members of each group. Each student now has three papers to read, closely and critically, noting down all thoughts and objections in the margins, and a few days are allotted for this purpose.

3. The groups then spend the next two class meetings discussing each paper among themselves. After these discussions, each student weighs the various critiques and incorporates those suggestions deemed worthy, producing a final draft of the paper.

4. This final draft is the only version submitted to the instructor and the only one to be graded.

A word on the reader's responsibilities is in order here. Each reader must attempt to approach each paper without a personal agenda. That is, if the author has chosen to deal with something about which you are ignorant, or which you regard as unimportant, you must not allow your inner biases to show. This goodwill is even more important for a paper with which the reader violently disagrees. The reader's entire function is to improve the paper, which—as an essay—is most likely a very personal statement from the author. In setting forth objections and offering improvements, you should exercise tact and diplomacy. Remember, as a colleague in the same class, each reviewer will both give and face evaluation, and you will want to show the same consideration you hope other reviewers will show your work.

In this exercise, the three peers in each author's group constitute a test audience for arguments, turns of phrase, organization, and quality of thought. These individuals stand in for a "general readership" more effectively than the professor can, and they provide different perspectives from which an essay may be evaluated. Student writers sometimes find such evaluation processes harrowing, but they also invariably find them beneficial.

The final draft of an essay (indeed, of any piece of writing) is a kind of performance. This is the version of your work presented for evaluation to the public—or to at least one reader—and this is the version that will leave a final impression. How many of us have thought ruefully, after a performance, "But it went *fine* in the practice room!"? In writing we are more fortunate; the "performance" does not happen in real time. The editing process is analogous, rather, to preparing a digital recording: all the wrong notes can be removed, all the phrasing can be recalibrated, all the awkward moments softened into excellence. In the editing process the "performer" can say "sorry; let me do that a bit better" with impunity as many times as necessary. For musicians that is an unimagined luxury.

But authors pay for this privilege with patience and time. Because most of the writing process consists of revision—writing being, in large part, a matter of rewriting—writing is a multistep process that cannot profitably be hurried. Fine writing requires good organization and a strong rough draft as building blocks, certainly, but most of all it requires persistent, patient editing, with much reading aloud and self-evaluation. In other words, you will produce many drafts, and your vigilance in critiquing them cannot flag. As this phase requires time and patience above all, it is necessary to get to it as soon as possible.

6

Research in Music

It is the rare music student indeed who rejoices at the announcement of a written assignment or term paper.[1]

—JOHN E. DRUESEDOW, JR.

Sharp lines of demarcation do not separate research papers, program notes, reviews, and critical essays; each of these genres utilizes both research and critical evaluation. The distinctions are of emphasis rather than of kind: an essay is primarily a persuasive exercise, but it needs to be based on facts; program notes are primarily a presentation of general background research targeted at the music lover rather than a more specialized reader; and the research paper is primarily a presentation of specific, academic research in coherent, digested form.

This chapter addresses the research process in music, from the choice of topic to the gathering of material, to organization, to written presentation.

THE PURPOSES OF RESEARCH

Students too often look upon the musical scholarship they read in books and journals as something to be neither questioned nor used as a model, seeing it instead as the intimidating product of higher, perhaps more boring but certainly wholly alien, intellects. Music researchers are wrongly

---

[1]John E. Druesedow, Jr., *Library Research Guide to Music* (Ann Arbor, MI: Pierian Press, 1982), 1.

perceived to be fundamentally separate from other musicians and the musical world. Researching, a skill that will prove invaluable in a musical lifetime, is thus feared and avoided. This is wrong, but widespread.

Far better is the idea of a continuum. There is no essential difference between student research and professional research, for they share the goal of enhancing the understanding of both researcher and readers. In a college course, this means the understanding of the student author-researcher, perhaps the class, and even the professor. (The professor may well learn something about the subject and will certainly learn about the student author's understanding of it.) When writing for publication, the goal is to enlighten a certain kind of reader: an article in a magazine will seek to enlighten one group of readers, and an article in a scholarly journal or book will aim at another group. But with all topics, from the most widely studied to the most obscure, each author offers something unique, and so may be said to make a contribution to the field, even when the contribution is simply a clear summary and presentation of others' published research. For the undergraduate, seeing yourself as a member of the broad authorial and research family enables you to identify more and more with the wider musical world and to find a place within it without limiting your view to the immediate environment of practice-room, classroom, or department.

CHOICE OF TOPIC

In many courses you will be assigned a topic or told to choose your own topic within assigned parameters. When you have no immediate affinity for your topic, don't be overpowered by resentment. Think of it the way you would think of practicing études, or learning or teaching repertoire that does not have your full sympathy. In performance, every work is your favorite work in the world, and every style has your most profound commitment. So it is with writing; regardless of the topic or the extent of your commitment, every stage of the process requires your absolute best.

If you do have leeway in choosing a topic, write about the subject matter that makes your heart beat fastest. Such a choice may involve a particular work or kind of music, a musical issue or question, or any of a number of related areas, but it is best to proceed from your own passion. The worst course of action is to choose a topic on the basis of what you think the professor would like to see, or the supposed ease of completion, or the simplicity of the issue involved. The goal of "justing getting it done" is no more acceptable than the goal of a barely passable performance of a Mozart piano concerto would be.

A common mistake is the choice of a topic that is too broad. While topics like "American Indian Music," "Chopin's Ornamentation," and "The Blues Roots of Rock and Roll" may initially seem promising, each has had at least several books devoted to it already. A research paper on one of these topics would only scratch the surface, and it would likely be a collection of somewhat random facts that do not lead in a particular direction. Far better to narrow the focus; for example, the first topic might become "An Overview of Navajo Music" or "Navajo Courtship Songs," depending on the researcher's background. The second might be narrowed to "The Influence of Operatic Ornamentation on Chopin," "Chopin's Ornamental Variants: Why?" or "How Is Chopin's Ornamentation To Be Played?" Promising subtopics derived from the third might include "Robert Johnson's Legacy in the Work of Eric Clapton and Led Zeppelin" or "The Relationship Between Blues and Rock Song Formats." Answering a specific how or why question, producing a comparison, or addressing some other specific task can focus research more easily than trying to produce an "overview" paper. Setting boundaries can help ensure that the researcher does not get lost well into the research process.

If a topic is too narrow, you can broaden the scope by expanding the time period in question, looking at related repertoire or additional composers, or asking different questions about the context in which the music under discussion appeared. Ultimately, whether a topic is too narrow or too broad depends in large part on the author's background and the length of the assignment. Self awareness and forethought are therefore indispensible tools in the early stages of research.

KINDS OF WRITTEN SOURCES

Publications about music (that is, books and articles), musical scores themselves, and sound recordings are all sources—sources to be used very differently—and these sources (and a great deal else) may be available in electronic form. Here are four truths regarding sources:

- there is a huge amount of source material available
- the number of sources is constantly growing
- no source is 100% dependable
- no single source is completely duplicated by another

It is safe neither to trust any single source implicitly nor to ignore any sources you have at your disposal. As many sources as possible must be critically examined. The task of the researcher is not only to be aware of and familiar with the relevant sources, but to be able to evaluate each and use it accordingly. (The idea of evaluation is discussed below.)

Non-English Sources

The reality in music is that research material directly relevant to your work is not always published in English. For this reason, the ability to access literature in foreign languages is a great advantage. The available English-language sources will usually be sufficient for most undergraduate research topics, although if you are studying a foreign language it would be a great idea to try your linguistic wings on a source or two in that language. For graduate-level research, or research intended for publication, access to foreign-language sources is a necessity, either through using your own skills (which always benefit from practice) or, less ideally, with the help of a friend or professional translator. Much depends on the topic: for example, virtually all the important sources on the Spanish composer Joaquín Rodrigo are in Spanish, so it is hard to imagine any research on him by someone with no capability in that language. By contrast, a good deal of the most important research on composers such as Bach and Mozart is written in English, so one could certainly say that it is as important for a German or Austrian researcher studying those composers to know English as it is for English and North American researchers to know German. The truth is that language skills are necessary for any ongoing work in music research. That said, we will proceed to a short survey of English-language sources.

Reference Sources

The first stop for any research project needs to be one (or more) of the major reference works in music. Among the benefits of this is the clarification of concepts central to your project but perhaps not all that common outside it (that is, the huge gray area between "common knowledge" and the specifics you will be researching); you want this to happen *before* the project is well under way. The information in standard reference works is the product, for the most part, of relatively recent scholarship (although, of course, our understanding deepens all the time, and no source is error-free). Bibliographies of relevant books and articles are often provided, offering a variety of fruitful places to look next.

The standard English-language music reference work is *The New Grove Dictionary of Music and Musicians*, edited by Stanley Sadie, in 20 volumes (London: Macmillan, 1980). More of an encyclopedia than a dictionary, this compendious work has had several spin-off series: the *New Grove Dictionary of Musical Instruments* (1984), the *New Grove Dictionary of American Music* (1986), the *New Grove Dictionary of Jazz* (1988), and the *New Grove Dictionary of Opera* (1992). (Many of the more substantial articles have been issued in revised form as separate volumes, either individually, as with Mozart, or in small anthologies, such as *High Renaissance Masters*.) For rock and pop music, there is a similar work: the *Encyclopedia of Popular Music*, third edition, compiled and edited by Colin Larkin, in eight volumes (New York: Muze UK, 1998). Musical terminology may be found in the *New Harvard Dictionary of Music*, third edition, edited by Don Randel (Cambridge, MA: Harvard University Press, 1986), and musicians and musical figures can be found in *Baker's Biographical Dictionary of Musicians*, eighth edition, edited by Nicolas Slonimsky (New York: Schirmer, 1992).

The preceding is only the shortest of short lists; further help on navigating the thousands of reference works available in music may be found by consulting Phillip D. Crabtree and Donald H. Foster, *Sourcebook for Research in Music* (Bloomington, IN: Indiana University Press, 1993), Vincent H. Duckles and Ida Reed, *Music Reference and Research Materials*, fifth edition (New York: Schirmer, 1997), or a good reference librarian. Even better, browse the reference shelf before consulting the librarian; first learn as much as you can on your own. It is wise not to approach a librarian unless you have already made a good-faith, intelligent effort to find at least the basic information yourself.

Books

Many articles in the *New Grove* dictionaries have bibliographies which list many helpful sources. But as of this writing, the *New Grove* is almost twenty years old. This is not to say that such a reference work becomes out of date in twenty years, but that the bibliographies will certainly lack important newer sources. (A new edition of *New Grove* is expected shortly, and then the cycle will begin again.) It is therefore probably a better plan to examine the recent sources before locating those in the *New Grove* bibliographies.

Before taking the next step, you need to have a solid familiarity with the music to be studied. It is expected, then, that you will already have the scores and have listened to recordings—ideally, several different recordings, so that you can compare them. Do not underestimate the importance of this step; your written sources may well assume that the reader is already familiar with the music, so using them before you have achieved this familiarity will only mean you have to return and read them again.

After you have perused the reference works and are familiar with the music, your next visit to the music library is likely to net you several books relevant to your topic. Let us say that you are studying Chopin's piano sonatas. You locate the Chopin section and immediately find a number of substantial-looking books, several of which (you learn from the tables of contents and indexes) have lengthy passages, or even entire chapters, on the sonatas. Given this bounty, you may be tempted to believe that you are done collecting material. But wait: completely different perspectives may await you in books on the sonata (in general), on Polish music (Chopin is Poland's most famous composer), and on Parisian piano music of the 1830s and 1840s (when Chopin resided in Paris), to name only three areas. So, in seeking out relevant books, it is necessary to approach a research topic from several directions. Often the most helpful information will be gleaned from books that initially seem to be only tangentially related to your topic.

Do not forget collections of correspondence, autobiographical material, and primary-source documentation. While an individual's first-person testimony may not be any more trustworthy than other sources (memories may fade, translations may mislead, and a particular version of a story may seem more attractive to the author than what actually happened), it offers yet another angle of approach to a musical work, person, or question. When a particular work is being studied, *always* look for it in the index to the composer's published correspondence, and even if it does not appear, read as much as possible on that portion of the composer's life.

Journal and Magazine Articles

Much of the periodical literature is *juried*, which means that before an article is published, it is read and approved by the editor of the magazine, or in the case of a scholarly journal by the editor and a small group of scholars—who often recommend revisions—to make sure it is dependable and meets the standards of the publication. This process does not guarantee the veracity of every word published, but the oversight does offer additional assurance of quality. With nonjuried publications such as many newsletters, quality is harder to establish; the articles in a newsletter can be entirely unjuried (and thus their veracity depends on the integrity of each individual author), or there may be substantial editorial oversight. Scholarly newsletters (such as the *Newsletter of the American Brahms Society*) tend to be as dependable as juried publications simply because they function as scholarly journals; they are usually produced by scholars and have scholarly contributions, but they serve the needs of a narrower group of readers than a journal would.

For all but the most superficial research projects, the periodical literature must be scoured for relevant articles. The same observations about directly and indirectly related book sources apply here, too, so for information on Brahms, for example, you would have to look at more periodicals than the *Newsletter of the American Brahms Society*, helpful and relevant though it will be. Other angles, in addition to scholarly theory and history journals, might include publications on piano music (if relevant; or chamber music, the symphony, etc.), nineteenth-century music, or theory and analysis. Sadly, music as a field does not enjoy some of the resources that other fields do. The entire historical periodical literature in some professions is almost completely indexed, and others have many of their publications available on-line. There is currently no single global database of the music periodical literature. For the last five decades, two sources are particularly helpful: *The Music Index: A Subject-Author Guide to Music Periodical Literature* (Detroit: Information Services, 1949-63; Detroit: Information Coordinators, 1963-87; Warren, MI: Harmonie Park Press [Information Coordinators], 1987-), and *RILM Abstracts of Music Literature/Répertoire internationale de la littérature musicale* (New York: International Musicological Society, the Association of Music Libraries, Archives, and Document Centers, and the International Council for Traditional Music, 1967-). *The Music Index* provides article citations for a wide variety of music periodicals, including review citations indexed by the subject of the review. *RILM Abstracts* provides citations and abstracts not only for periodical articles, but for books on music, master's theses, and doctoral dissertations. There are databases other than these, but they tend to be more specialized; it will probably be most helpful for student researchers to proceed first from these sources, and from citations in others' bibliographies, until they become familiar with the research tools available.

Recording Liner Notes

Almost all sound recordings come with some kind of explanatory material, and there is nothing wrong (in principle) with utilizing it in the research process. That said, a warning of *caveat lector* ("Let the reader beware") is in order. While many recordings have excellent notes, others do not; authors can be crippled by the limited space provided or told to write on a *very* general level. Perhaps the recording company felt that liner notes were not important enough to hire a competent author in the first place (this was more the case with older recordings than with more recent ones). Notes often tend to be general, rightly targeted at the music-purchasing public rather than a research audience, so they cannot serve as the backbone source of a project. Still, helpful information is sometimes to be found in these sources. With practice, you will develop good instincts about the quality of what you read.

Web-Based Sources

The World Wide Web is making an ever-increasing amount of material available in this, the so-called Information Age. Some of this material duplicates or updates (with much greater convenience) print resources such as *RILM Abstracts* and *Music Index*, both of which exist in electronic formats. In addition, the *International Index of Music Periodicals* (Chadwyck-Healey, Inc.) is an extremely useful searchable database, with brief abstracts as well as citations for articles on musical subjects. Access to these databases is by subscription, and subscribers are usually such institutions as university libraries. These databases should only be consulted in addition to print resources, not as an alternative. To my knowledge, no database exhaustively duplicates another.

Web pages may be owned and administered by anyone with access to the required computer resources: a company, an organization, a scholar, a hobbyist, any private individual. A tremendous amount of information may be found on web pages, the format of which lends itself to people with specific, somewhat narrow interests. Despite the amount of information readily available, because websites are unjuried, the *caveat lector* warning is doubly appropriate: variations in quality and dependability can be extreme.

Musical Scores

Almost any research on a musical topic requires the examination of musical scores. All scores are not, however, created equal; different kinds of scores are produced with different purposes in mind. More discussion of this point follows in Use of Sources, below; for now it will suffice to describe several varieties of scores.

An *Urtext* is an edition that seeks to transmit, as faithfully and exactly as possible, what the composer put on the manuscript page and/or what appeared in the earliest editions, those under the composer's control, without editorial intrusions of any kind. Frequently the explanatory notes of the urtext address variant readings and differences between sources. A *performance edition* provides not only the composer's score but an editor's recommendations for performance. These may include (in addition to whatever indications the composer provided) suggestions on phrasing, fingering, bowing, articulation, ornamentation, and general performance instructions and metronome marks. (A hybrid is the scholarly performance edition, which seeks to marry scholarly accuracy of the score with informed recommendations regarding historical performance practices.) *Study scores* are generally low-budget reprints of earlier editions (miniature scores fall into this category); their goal is to make available a maximum amount of music for the minimum cost. They are intended neither as performing editions nor as last-word scholarly documents. *Collected works* editions, found primarily in libraries, seek to include a composer's entire output in a single, multivolume edition. Related to collected works are *monumental editions,* also intended primarily for libraries, which include generally hard-to-find works by a variety of composers. Famous examples of monumental sets include *Denkmäler der Tonkunst in Österreich* (Monuments of Musical Art in Austria) and *Musica Britannica.* Scholarly accuracy is a central goal of both collected works and monumental editions, but since scholars continue working in these areas, the accuracy of this work tends to come under debate relatively quickly.

For learning the contents of collected works and monumental editions, the best source is still Anna Harriet Heyer, *Historical Sets, Collected Editions, and Monuments of Music* (Chicago: American Library

Association, 1980), in two volumes. A newer version, edited by George Hill and Norris Stephens, appeared in 1997, but this version is much less helpful because it does not list the contents of each monumental set. I recommend the earlier version, good at least for monumental editions published before 1980. When this information is all available electronically, as Hill and Stephens suggest it will be, that will undoubtedly be the most efficient format.

USE OF SOURCES

Optimizing Research Time. Working intelligently is far better than working hard. As you go through your steadily increasing pile of sources, you may begin to suspect that it will be impossible to complete your project (or any project) before the due date, or for that matter before your graduation! Just to read six available biographies would take more time than you have. Isn't there, you wonder, a better way?

This is where a revelation occurs: you do not need to read, word for word, every source that looks like it may have something promising. Skimming sources for relevant material is one of the researcher's most essential skills. When you research a particular piece or pieces, start with a basic understanding of the composer's biography (such as may be found in *New Grove* or in a recent published biography) and then proceed to tables of contents and indexes, looking for information on your piece. Find the years in which the piece was composed and examine the passages dealing with that time period for relevant information. The same is true when you research a person or a problem rather than a particular piece; save time by using safe, dependable shortcuts.

Don't Believe Everything You Read! This advice, *caveat lector,* is as valuable today as it has ever been. Virtually every source, from the most scholarly to the most popularized, contains errors. Unfortunately, authors have different standards of accuracy, and while a book's main area of focus may be rigorously documented and presented, ancillary material may be somewhat more casually handled. You may doubt that a student would be able to judge the merit of published works (or even have the gall to attempt it), but you are well within your rights and capabilities in learning to do so.

Imagine that you want to do a research paper on a favorite 1960s rock group, and you find the group discussed in great detail in a book that seeks to prove that rock is the greatest evil of the twentieth century, the pernicious product of hostile foreign influences, the devil, or both. (Such books do exist.) Would you trust the author's comments about your favorite group? Must you, because this book is in print, quote it on your subject and treat its content as fact, or at least as worth addressing? To choose a less extreme example, imagine that you are interested in, say, the masses of a certain Renaissance composer. You find contradictory information in two books, one a general history of Western music, the other a more specialized study of this composer's works. You must ask: when were the two sources written? And which is more likely to be right? You will have to check additional sources in hopes of identifying the error and avoiding it, whoever made it. And this leaves aside the different interpretive conclusions, presented with due authorial assurance, that will be drawn by different writers about the same musical works or music-related issues. While there is no surefire method, particularly for students, for evaluating unfamiliar sources, the principles explained above will aid in this process and will enable your research instincts to become ever more dependable.

Scholarly vs. Textbook Sources. A researcher needs to examine sources while bearing in mind the goals of each. General sources and more specialized scholarly sources differ in a variety of ways, and they cannot be understood as equivalent. For example, one standard general history textbook states, "The vocal forms of the Renaissance were marked by smoothly gliding melodies conceived for the voice."[2] What does the student researcher then make of some of the early secular vocal works of the fifteenth-century composer Guillaume Du Fay, which can be highly syncopated, rhythmically complex, and difficult enough to require a virtuoso vocal technique? What of the sometimes frenetic and mercurial melodic lines of the late-Renaissance madrigals of Carlo Gesualdo? But these counterexamples do not disprove the fact that, in general, a good part of the Renaissance vocal aesthetic had to do with

---

[2]Joseph Machlis and Kristine Forney, *The Enjoyment of Music*, 7th ed., Chronological version (New York: W. W. Norton, 1995), 99.

smoothness, seamlessness, and the creation of melodies that were not only gratifying to sing but resonated well within the acoustic spaces of churches and cathedrals, where voices were frequently heard.

Remember, general sources provide a *general* background; they set the stage for further work by presenting a broad overall context, but they cannot be read as if their information were as specifically true as that in specialized studies. This caveat applies also to articles in periodicals; the goals and approach of (for example) an article appearing in a magazine for piano teachers must be kept in mind when comparing its contents with those of an article in a research journal.

Relative Age of Sources. Although certain older souces such as Manfred Bukofzer's *Music in the Baroque Era*[3] remain immensely valuable, it is risky to rely on them because their authors had no access to recent research. Older sources may also reflect antiquated and parochial perspectives. But reliance on modern sources, too, carries risks. Modern sources may be shaped and informed by fashionable but ephemeral critical or aesthetic perspectives, and (particularly with relatively recent sources) are further removed from historical subjects than older sources are. So, while we may be properly cautious of older sources' presumed narrowness and antiquation, modern sources can themselves be firmly and confidently based on cultural suppositions alien to the subject in question.

The positive side of this two-part warning is that both older and more modern sources have, at least potentially, specific strengths. Older sources are closer to the worldview and zeitgeist of the music of recent centuries, and they may have the benefit of more oral history (such as authors' interviews with people involved with or witness to the music, person, or issue under discussion). Further, an older source may be the product of a mind so insightful that it remains valuable no matter what particulars are altered by subsequent research. (The writings of Donald Francis Tovey and, again, Manfred Bukofzer come to mind.) Modern sources usually aspire to modern scholarly standards, seek to take all source material and previous research into account, and aim to arrive at critical conclusions based on evidence, and this may well make them more dependable and inclusive than earlier efforts.

---

[3]Manfred Bukofzer, *Music in the Baroque Era* (New York: W. W. Norton, 1947).

How much of this is true for each source will vary. The only general-izations it is safe to make are that the age of a source informs what and how it is able to communicate, and all sources must be used by re-searchers with a critical stance in mind.

Authorial Perspective. The evaluation of not only authors but their agendas is a vital task for the researcher, who seeks above all not to be misled. A modern reader will be surprised to find conversations among long-dead historical figures and detailed descriptions of historical events in certain older sources—and even in some newer ones—and still may (mistakenly) consider such sources trustworthy. Some decades ago, fabri-cating conversations and other historical details in order to produce a "good read" was acceptable; in fact, it is safe to consider any such mater-ial suspect. Similar are those cases where the authors of books and arti-cles approach a subject from a specific polemical position, such as that the essence of Chopin's character may be seen in his religious beliefs,[4] or that rock music is habitually laced with subliminal messages that range from commercially manipulative to satanic,[5] or that Arnold Schoenberg's views of the "emancipation of dissonance" were based on poor history and a personal agenda.[6] Authors who approach their musical subjects from the perspective of proving such all-encompassing points are best viewed from a distance. Their goals are narrow, and the accuracy of their supporting material is frequently of secondary importance.

Dependability of the Source Itself. The more research one does, the more one develops a sense about the dependability of sources. Many people love music, many people produce it in some way, and (more to the point) many write about it, regardless of training, knowledge, or any other standard prerequisite. Music is a subject about which people with no training or personal experience often feel they have a good deal to say simply because it gives them pleasure. Books and articles by both the

---

[4]Mateusz Gliński, *Chopin the Unknown* (Windsor, ONT: Assumption University of Windsor Press, 1963).

[5]Dan and Steve Peters, with Cher Merrill, *Rock's Hidden Persuader: The Truth about Backmasking* (Minneapolis: Bethany House, 1985).

[6]William Thomson, *Schoenberg's Error* (Philadelphia: University of Pennsylvania Press, 1991).

trained and the untrained may seem credible on first examination, regardless of whether the writings have had appropriate evaluation, editorial guidance, or oversight before publication.

For all its potential benefits, the World Wide Web is even more problematic. The democratization of information—anyone can set up a website and say virtually anything—makes it incumbent upon researchers to be as critical as possible of the information they pick up. Many websites are owned and administered by private citizens, and any monitoring for quality or accuracy is up to them. There is nothing to prevent a junior high or high school student from deciding to put everything she or he knows about the blues on a website—nor should there be—but the danger lies in a college student's credulity in the information found there. It is easy to assume that anyone who takes the trouble to write, either on paper or on the Web, knows something about the subject, but nothing could be further from the truth. This is why "I picked this up off the Web" is one of the least convincing defenses for any otherwise undefended information. It is not that information on private websites is automatically wrong; it is that there is nothing to *prevent* it from being wrong, and that it is necessary to corroborate it with other sources. Again, although there are no guarantees, juried sources are always potentially more dependable than nonjuried ones.

Special Difficulties in Using Musical Sources. In using and evaluating any source, it is always necessary to keep the focus of the project itself in clear view. This focus, more than anything else, will facilitate the accurate assessment of the source's relevance or authority for the purposes at hand. Sources may be virtually unimpeachable in terms of their intended uses, but through misuse or misinterpretation they may still lead the novice researcher astray. Among those most often misused are musical scores.

Let us say that a student researcher wants to establish, as closely as possible, how J. S. Bach believed a particular sarabande for keyboard ought to be performed. Should this student go to the original manuscript or to an *Urtext,* a presumably faithful reproduction (in published form) of the score, exactly as the composer notated the work? The premise here would be that the score alone is as complete today as it was in Bach's time, that anything that Bach did not explicitly notate, a modern performer need not know. Is this a safe assumption for music written between 250 and 300 years ago? We know that there were performance conventions that musicians of Bach's time would have known and practiced, from specific and idiomatic rhythmic realizations (such as *notes inégales*) to ways of ornamenting (for example, on repeats) and of achieving dynamic variation using the different manuals of a harpsichord. Neither the composer's manuscript nor a published *Urtext* would provide any of this information, and a student researcher would be dangerously underinformed.

Is our student better off, then, with an edited musical score? Perhaps, perhaps not. Editors can provide explanatory notes and informed suggestions for phrasings, fingerings, ornamentation, and other matters, but they can also mislead by such prescriptions. A keyboard fingering conceived by a pianist today for digital ease might completely confound another player's hand, the phrasing of the period, and in any case be unworkable on a harpsichord, clavichord, or organ (the keyboard instruments of Bach's time). Suggested ornamentation in Baroque or Classic music, about which there is always much debate, might be far too conservative or too florid. What is more, our understanding of Baroque phrasing, fingering, and other performance considerations has changed a great deal since many highly edited nineteenth-century performance editions (such as those of Adolf Ruthardt) were produced, and it continues to change. The most recent available edition, then? Maybe, but who is to say that that one editor had all the answers? One recent edition of J. S. Bach's *Well-Tempered Clavier* so carefully and thoroughly provided all kinds of information that it was extremely difficult to use.[7] Moral: *nothing* is completely safe or completely dependable. The researcher arrives at the information needed by constantly interrogating the sources, asking of each source only the questions appropriate to it, finding other sources for the unanswered questions, collecting and collating information, and drawing interpretive conclusions based on the critical appraisal of all available information.

Recordings, too, offer less "proof" than they sometimes seem to. It is tempting, particularly for students, to feel that a particular point about a work is "proven"—how much ornamentation to use, what tempo is appropriate—by a persuasive recording, particularly if it is by a famous artist or ensemble. But an individual recording "proves" very little about

---

[7]J. S. Bach, *The Well-Tempered Clavier*, vol. I, ed. Willard Palmer (Sherman Oaks, CA: Alfred Publishing, 1981).

a work. In one way, it is like a live performance: x amount of ornamentation may be appropriate, but the recording "proves" only that it worked *in this one performance*. Traditional, non-historically-informed readings of Baroque works may seem persuasive, and indeed the performers' artistry may make them so, but this does not "prove" anything about how the music is to be performed.

That music has been interpreted and recorded a certain way is no assurance that this is the way the music was conceived. For example, Eubie Blake's recording of Scott Joplin's *Maple Leaf Rag* is a great piece of playing and a fascinating historical document, but it tells us far more about Blake and his background and taste than about Joplin and the classic piano rag. The same can be said of Vladimir Horowitz's recordings of Chopin, and of any number of other recorded performances. Recordings, even those *by* a composer or made under the composer's control, have few prescriptive applications. The critical acumen of the listener, and the ability to read a score and understand musical context, are of primary importance in using recordings.

There are, then, far more questions to be asked than there are answers to be depended upon. This is a good thing! While it may initially make the research process seem intimidating, even impossible, what it really indicates is that research is a living, vibrant activity. Important materials are always being discovered, important issues are always benefiting from reframed questions, more insightful consideration, and new perspectives. Not only do we learn more daily, we consider and reflect with more skill and wisdom daily. There are no closed books in musical research, no questions that are so settled they do not need to be revisited.

CITING YOUR SOURCES

Few research issues are as important as the proper use and citation of your sources. Citations enable you to tell the reader which of the ideas in your work originated with someone else, and where they might be found. (Citation forms are found in Chapter 9.) It is no crime to base your work on that of others; virtually every piece of research is founded, one way or another, on research that came before. But the failure to cite sources, which amounts to taking credit for another's thoughts, whether intentional or inadvertent, whether the material is directly quoted or paraphrased, is *plagiarism*. Plagiarism is a crime in the publishing world and an actionable offense in colleges and universities, where standard penalties range from an automatic failing grade in the course to more lasting disciplinary action, including expulsion. Dishonesty is unforgivable; unfortunately, in matters of citation, carelessness is often indistinguishable from dishonesty. There is no margin for error in issues of academic integrity.

But does an author need to footnote every thought not explicitly his or her own? Of course not. All direct quotes require citation, as do specific facts that lie outside so-called common knowledge, such as: "In the Yardbirds' 'Heart Full of Soul,' Jeff Beck based his guitar hook on the playing of a sitarist who was on an earlier take." Whether the writer has heard one of the outtakes from the recording session or read this fact somewhere, it needs to be cited. But matters of common knowledge should not be cited, even when they are new to novice researchers. This is a gray area, and not all authorities or writing instructors agree on what constitutes common knowledge, or on how rigorous student authors need to be. (As always, your instructor's preferences prevail in this matter.) Consider this sentence:

> George Gershwin was born in 1898 to immigrant parents in New York City, and began his musical career at a New York publishing house, playing through songs for prospective interpreters.

The information contained in such a sentence need not be cited, because it is available in countless biographical treatments of the composer and is neither new nor debatable. If you were to quote the sentence directly, you would certainly have to cite the source because the words would not be your own, but there is no reason that this sort of sentence should be quoted rather than paraphrased.

To Quote or to Paraphrase? You will most often be quoting primary sources, such as historical documents or the comments or reminiscences of historical figures. Such direct quotations are splendid for making or supporting a point, but you should never assume that they need no explanation. What seems to you like an obvious connection may strike the reader as a non sequitur, so you must always provide commentary. Paraphrasing is best for secondary sources (such as articles or books by scholars). Secondary sources should only be quoted when you want to discuss or take specific issue with an author's formulation or view of the subject, such as when you need to address Donald Francis Tovey's view of

Beethoven's Fourth Piano Concerto rather than the concerto itself. Matters of fact, such as the sentence about Gershwin above, should be paraphrased, whether common knowledge or not.

TURNING RESEARCH INTO WRITING

The Foundations of Your Research. While the research process is in one sense never-ending, it does need to come to some kind of conclusion so that you may begin to write your paper. At the point you begin to write, you should feel ready to do so: both formative and specific research are completed, and you are not only prepared to view your subject in a proper context but also to arrive at some conclusions as a result of evaluating the evidence. Inevitably, minor points will still crop up, and you will have to look things up throughout the writing process. But waiting until the research process is as complete as possible before you begin to write will help ensure that your overview of the subject will not undergo radical changes.

That confidently said, it is common for an important source or a major piece of information to pop up unexpectedly during the writing process—perhaps a late arrival from Interlibrary Loan, perhaps a professor's offhand comment that points to a new direction, perhaps a realization of your own. Major revising and recasting, unforeseen and unscheduled, may well be necessary. There is no comfort in such cases other than remembering that this kind of semi-emergency is often a normal part of the process; all researchers, from students to professionals, know that research projects adapt themselves unwillingly to due dates and that inconveniences do occur.

From the point of completed research to writing, the process is much like that of essay writing (discussed in Chapter 5). You will need an outline, some kind of visual representation of the organization of your paper. The ordering and presentation of your premises, evidence, and conclusions, so that everything follows smoothly without causing doubt or giving pause, require time and reflection, and probably experimentation with more than one arrangement.

From here, it is a matter of *Sitzfleisch,* the padding on your coccyx bone. Good writing results not only from attention to the basics—preparation, outline, knowledge of readership, and the stylistic elements we discuss in Chapter 8—but also from *revising,* the process of repeatedly reading your own writing, learning to identify and improve wordy passages, unclear transitions, and other faults. It is because of the importance of revision that I encourage authors to write on a computer or word processor; large blocks of information and lengthy passages of writing are easily manipulated this way. You should expect to go through several drafts (a much more efficient process on a computer), and you will need to print at least two drafts *before* the final one; editing on paper is far more dependable than editing on the screen. The usual advice applies: write doggedly; if you get hung up, go on to something else; do not finish the opening and concluding paragraphs until the rest of the paper is done. Above all, *tell your story*. No amount of pseudo-academic writing will save a research paper in which the author has lost interest, or in which the research process was wrongly or incompletely carried out.

On Being Derivative. Many students and other fledgling authors fear being derivative, or basing their entire papers on others' research. But early in a research career (an undergraduate research paper is about as early as it is possible to be) one does not have much experience to draw upon. The research process happens from the ground up: background and specifics have to be acquired as part of this process. (If you continue doing projects in a particular field, you will be building on previously acquired knowledge; you will not have to keep starting anew.) Your first research papers must therefore be based largely on the work of others, primarily or exclusively on secondary sources. Nothing is wrong with this; solid experience using secondary sources is a prerequisite for being able to do primary research.

WHOSE IDEAS?

You may wonder how one can pass off research based on the work of others as one's own. Keep these points in mind:

- *you* chose which sources to use
- *you* have thoroughly assimilated the material from these sources and paraphrased and reworded to the point that there is no possibility of plagiarism
- the conclusions *you* drew from these sources are your own

Choice of Sources. In choosing certain sources over others, trusting one perspective rather than another (sometimes called "privileging"), researchers make decisions for which they can be held responsible. That is, were someone to ask why one source was prefered to another, the writer of the research paper should be able to provide an answer. What seems to be "merely" a presentation of information culled from other sources is therefore far more than that; the author, in choosing the sources and deciding what information to consider relevant from each, has shaped the study and made it something unique, not merely a rehash.

Conclusions. The end of a research paper must not only follow logically from the coherent presentation of evidence and argument; it must also demonstrate understanding and mastery of the subject of the paper. It is impossible to do this—to conclude, summarize, tie up in a neat package—without stating some kind of opinion.

Here is the concluding paragraph from a student research paper, "Folk Songs in the Music of Ralph Vaughan Williams," by Matthew Larson. The paper goes into some detail regarding Vaughan Williams's folk song collecting activities, his lifelong love of the folk idiom, and the ways in which he used both actual folk songs and more general elements from the English musical language—melodic modes, altered scale degrees, melodies that emphasize first and fifth scale degrees, and so on. In conclusion, Mr. Larson writes:

> Vaughan Williams once quoted Gilbert Murray as saying,
> "The original genius is at once the child of tradition and a rebel
> against it."[8] Williams himself was both a child of the cosmopolitan
> musical tradition he was born into and a rebel against it. His
> dedication to producing uniquely English music, his thorough
> knowledge of foreign music, and his loyalty to his own art made
> him the father of the twentieth-century school of composition in
> England. "He recreated an English musical vernacular, thereby
> enabling the next generation to take their nationality for
> granted . . ."[9] The next generation of English composers, even

---

[8][Larson's note] Ralph Vaughan Williams, *The Making of Music* (New York: Cornell University Press, 1955), 52.

[9][Larson's note] Hugh Ottaway, "Vaughan Williams, Ralph," *The New Grove Dictionary of Music and Musicians* (London: Macmillan, 1980), vol. 19, 577.

> though they rebelled against it, could not help but be influenced
> and satisfied by the music Vaughan Williams revived. Without his
> work, English music would be nothing more than a hodgepodge of
> quotations from the music of other nations.

The wording here is rather strong; a couple of things are said that might better not have been. "Quotations" is the wrong word, and it is a bit insulting to suggest that the absence of any one individual would have resulted in a nation's music being a "hodgepodge." (The author might have done better without the last sentence entirely.) But for our purposes, this is beside the point. Mr. Larson has summarized what he wants the reader to take from his presentation of evidence—that Ralph Vaughan Williams's use of folk songs and of individual musical elements therefrom changed the character of English music for the entire century. He presents this not as fact but as his opinion, based on his evaluation of the music and sources he examined. His use of quoted material for context and to strengthen his point is effective and elegant. His conclusions are thus wholly appropriate for a research paper.

Concluding a paper is not easy, and avoiding certain common pitfalls requires caution. One often-used type of conclusion refuses to take a stand or calls for further research. The motivations for this sort of non-opinion are obvious, and they are not always wrong: caution in taking too risky a stand, or humility in not wanting to consider one's own research effort as the last word on a subject. But the net effect of such a conclusion is to undermine the entire paper that led to it. Consider the following closing sentence:

> But only the future can tell if atonal music will gain ascendancy or if
> tonality will stage a comeback.

Conclusions like this fabricated example, which I call "the-future-remains-to-be-seen conclusions," are ultimately unhelpful in that they suggest nothing more than a shrug of the author's shoulders. Further, in the vague statement of an oppositional possibility, they frequently mask the deeper and more interesting possibilities that might merit discussion—in this case, say, the yet unimagined musical possibilities that are neither tonal nor atonal, or the coexistence of tonal and atonal music (which is what we currently enjoy). The kind of conclusion parodied above provides one thing: an excuse for a not-too-graceful exit, which is always something to avoid.

Another inelegant leave-taking is the sort of conclusion that begins, "But these results can only be considered preliminary until further research investigates (corroborates, establishes, etc.). . . ." The researcher wants to communicate that he or she understands proper research method, that all the problems in the field will not be solved by this single paper, that certain kinds of results need to be reproduceable. These cautions are responsible and laudable. However, the message communicated by such a statement drastically weakens the overall effect of the research. What it seems to say is "Unfortunately, what you have just read cannot really stand on its own. Only when others do something related to this can we have any confidence in the study you have just completed reading." This is not the way to conclude a piece of research.

Finally, there are the time-honored summations, "in conclusion, this music was so influential that it led, ultimately, to the music of today," and "this music is so great it will survive eternally." Conclusions of this sort indicate two things: 1) the author has no idea what a conclusion ought to be, and 2) he or she at least wants to acknowledge that the music is important, somehow. These, too, are utterly insufficient conclusions.

The best way to approach conclusions, when one is having difficulty wrapping up, is to reread the paper several times (always a good idea in any case) in order to recapture a *global* sense of where it has been leading. Firm conclusions based on that, even if highly personal ("All this documentary material leads me to believe . . ."), are always more persuasive than an unwillingness to take any position at all or a plaintive call for further research. Particularly on the undergraduate level, the paper may well be leading toward an assertion about which there is little disagreement—"It seems clear that Chopin composed the most accomplished Nocturnes of the 1830s and 1840s"—but such conclusions have presumably been prepared and backed up by the paper itself and are therefore sufficiently strong and appropriate.

Returning to Mr. Larson's conclusions, we note again how "authorial" they are, how they represent a personal position that results from the information presented. Larson's conclusion nicely illustrates a central point: no matter how extensively other sources have been used in a music research paper, it remains a very personal and subjective kind of project, and the author is not only present but responsible for the sources chosen and examined and the conclusions drawn. The responsibilities are great; because many skills are necessary in assembling a persuasive, informative presentation of research, research projects are among the most work-intensive writing projects in the musical field. When mastered, though, these skills prove useful in all areas of endeavor.

7

A Sample Research Paper in Music

On the following pages is a complete research paper by an undergraduate student, Tim Sullivan, a senior theory-composition major. This paper is titled "Similar Processes, Different Results: Development in the Piano Works of György Ligeti." As you read it, note the variety of sources, the use of musical examples, and the author's approach to gleaning information and drawing conclusions. Note also the author's attention to the citations and the bibliography.

The University of Northern Colorado

Similar Processes, Different Results:

Development in the Piano Works of György Ligeti

Tim Sullivan

MUS 152: Writing in the Performing and Visual Arts

Prof. Bellman

Spring, 1998

Similar Processes, Different Results: Development in the
Piano Works of György Ligeti

by Tim Sullivan

György Ligeti is a maverick among living composers. He has
managed to distance himself from both the "academic" composers
and the "neo-romantic" composers, which is a feat few have
accomplished. He embraces modern scientific thought, yet never
allows its influence to dominate at the expense of musical
creativity. He has either originated, or at the least experimented
with, nearly every recent compositional development, but has
never settled into any one "style." Ligeti's imagination, curiosity,
and ability to change have extended through five decades of
artistic production, which has resulted in a body of works that,
similar to Stravinsky's, displays striking originality and contrast.

Born in 1923 to Hungarian-Jewish parents, Ligeti began
studying the piano at age fourteen. Ironically, it was his younger
brother who was considered to possess the greater musical talent.
Unfortunately, this talent was not realized, for both Ligeti's father
and brother were killed in Auschwitz during World War II. Ligeti is
by no means a concert pianist (according to him, one must start
before puberty to develop a clean technique),[1] but the piano is his
primary instrument. It is also the instrument that he has most often

---

[1]György Ligeti, notes to *György Ligeti: Works for Piano*
(György Ligeti Edition 3, 1996), CD, Sony Classical SK 62308, 7-8.

1

used to try out new ideas. Because of this, a study of his piano works will illustrate nearly all of his compositional development (with the notable exception of the "micropolyphony" works).[2]

After WWII, Ligeti went to Budapest to study composition with Ferenc Farkas and Sandor Veress at the Budapest Academy. It was at this time that Ligeti composed *Capriccio No. 1* (1947), *Invention* (1948), and *Capriccio No. 2* (1947), all for solo piano. Ligeti has stated that he considers the two capriccios to be the most successful and the most personal works of his student years.[3]

As will be demonstrated, many of his later compositional breakthroughs found their beginnings in these three student pieces.

---

[2]This paper will focus on the piano music of György Ligeti which is currently in print. This includes: *Capriccio No. 1; Invention; Capriccio No. 2; Musica Ricercata; Monument, Selbstportrait, Bewegung; Études pour piano—premier livre;* and the *Konzert für Klavier und Orchester.* Omitted are: *Études pour piano—second livre* and some student pieces written before 1047, all of which have been recorded, but are not yet published. Refer to *György Ligeti: Works for Piano* (György Ligeti Edition 3, 1996), CD, Sony Classical SK 62308, and *György Ligeti: Keyboard Works* (György Ligeti Edition 6, 1997), CD, Sony Classical SK 62307, for recordings, and to Robert W. Richart, *György Ligeti: A Bio-Bibliography* (New York: Greenwood Press, 1990), for a complete list of works.

[3]Amy Bauer, "György Ligeti: *Capriccio Nr. 1 (1947); Invention (1948); Capriccio Nr. 2 (1947) für Klavier,*" *Notes* 51/3 (March 1995), 1151.

2

Capriccio No. 1, a short piece in a modified sonata form, shows the influence of Bartók, who remained Ligeti's idol until 1950.[4] This is apparent here through Ligeti's consistent use of bi-tonality and bi-modality. Also, similar to Bartók and Stravinsky, Ligeti used small melodic cells to compose much of his early music, especially in *Capriccio No. 2.* Upon graduation from the Budapest Academy, Ligeti obtained a grant to do field study of Hungarian and Rumanian folk music, in the tradition of Bartók and Kodály. He did this for one year, after which he returned to the Budapest Academy, this time as a professor of harmony and counterpoint.

With *Musica Ricercata* (1951–53), Ligeti "began formulating the basis of his mature style by restricting himself to purely musical considerations."[5] In this eleven-movement piece Ligeti extended cell composition to its limit, which resulted in the creation of an independent twelve-tone system (the music of Schoenberg, and most other Western music, was unavailable in Hungary at this time).[6] The first movement uses only the A in different octaves, with a D appearing at the very end of the movement.[7] The second

---

[4]T. Szitha, "A Conversation with György Ligeti," *Hungarian Music Quarterly* 3/1 (1992), 14; quoted in Mike Searby, "Ligeti the Postmodernist?," *Tempo* 199 (January 1, 1997), 9.

[5]John Warnaby, "Ligeti at 70," *Musical Opinion* 116 (May 1993), 152.

[6]Richart, 4.

[7]The seventh étude in Elliott Carter's *Eight Etudes and a Fantasy for Woodwind Quintet* (1950) is also composed using only

3

movement uses three notes, the third movement four notes, etc., until the eleventh and final movement uses all twelve notes.

It was through *Musica Ricercata* that Ligeti entered the ranks of avant-garde composers. Perhaps due to the cultural "freeze" in Hungary at the time, or maybe due to his desire to break away from academic composition, Ligeti had adopted an essentially radical approach to composition. He wanted to "discover what could be achieved with a single note, a single interval, a single chord."[8] At the same time, however, he continued to use bi-tonality and bi-modality in *Musica Ricercata* (ex. 1). In fact, Ligeti has continued to use these

Ex. 1. *Musica Ricercata*, VIII, m.15

techniques in his recent works, most notably in the first piano étude, "Désordre" (ex. 2), and in the first movement of the *Piano Concerto*.

Ligeti has also continued to broaden his preoccupation with rhythm in his later works, a fascination that is apparent even in his

---

one note. Ligeti would not have been aware of this work until at least 1956. Refer to Richart, 4.

[8]Warnaby, 152.

4

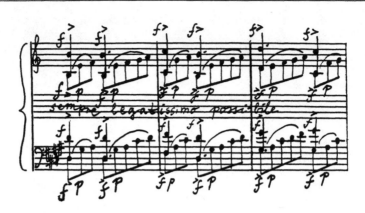

Ex. 2. "Désordre," beginning

earliest works. As a student, Ligeti often used Bulgarian rhythms in a manner similar to Bartók. The best example of this is *Capriccio No. 2,* which has a metric pattern of 5/8, 5/8, 7/8, 8/8. More recent examples occur in two of the piano études from book one.[9] The fourth piano étude, "Fanfares," uses a Bulgarian metrical structure, in this case 3/8, 2/8, 3/8. The ostinato in "Fanfares," comprised of two identical tetrachords a tritone apart, is absolutely unflinching, with exact repetitions (except for octave displacement) in every measure (ex. 3). The other hand (the ostinato constantly shifts between hands) plays the fanfares, which are rapid, consonant chordal figures. The fanfares usually conflict metrically with the

---

[9]As noted previously (see footnote 1), Ligeti has composed a second book of piano études, and has completed the first étude of a projected book three.

5

Ex. 3. "Fanfares," beginning

ostinato, creating all sorts of polyrhythms. Even with the simple ostinato, and the consonant fanfares, this piece remains radical "through sheer speed and rhythmic intricacy."[10]

"Désordre," the aforementioned first étude, is one of only two compositions which Ligeti has deliberately based on a mathematical concept. "Désordre" is self-similar, an iterated structure based consciously on the "Koch snowflake" (figs. 1 and 2).[11] Ligeti accomplishes this representation (it is not strict in the manner of Xenakis) through the combination of Bulgarian rhythms with the concept of overlaying grids. Each hand starts with the metric structure of 3+5, 3+5, 5+3, but the right hand gradually shifts along its grid, losing one eighth-note every fourth bar. At the same time, the phrase length in both hands is slowly reduced until

---

[10]Richard Steinitz, "The Dynamics of Disorder," *Musical Times* 137/1839 (May 1996), 11.

[11]Steinitz, "Dynamics," 8, 10. Steinitz explains: "The 'Koch curve,' proposed in 1904 by the Swedish mathematician Helge von Koch," results from an operation "in which smaller and smaller equilateral triangles are erected over the middle third of shorter and shorter straight lines. Starting out with a triangle and iterating this process produces the 'Koch snowflake.'"

6

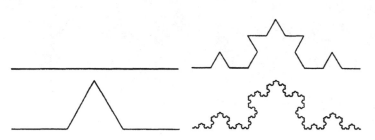

Fig. 1. The "Koch curve"

Fig. 2. The "Koch snowflake"

there is nothing left but metric accents. At this point, the grids have been completely worked through, but this only represents the first half. In order for this piece to be self-similar, the grids must be worked through the opposite way. The patterns start again, but this time, the left hand gains an eighth-note every fourth bar.

Ligeti first developed the concept of overlaying grids with the composition of *Monument,* the first of three pieces for two pianos, all of which were written in 1976. In connection with *Monument,* Ligeti has described the idea of "overlaying grids which, one after the other gradually change across the parameters of pitch, tempo, dynamics, and register."[12]

---

[12]Ligeti quoted in Christopher Bodman, "Darmstadt International Summer Course for New Music 1976," *Composer* 59 (Winter 1976/77), 31.

The first piano begins with a grid of A, Maestoso, fortissimo, and low-middle octave. Shortly after, the second piano enters with a grid of F-sharp, Maestoso, fortissimo, and low-middle octave. Slowly, Ligeti superimposes other grids on top of the existing ones. After all of the grids have run their course, all that remains is a single repeated note, the highest C on the piano, which both pianos repeat in sixteenth-notes until the end.

The full title of the second of the three pieces for two pianos is *Selbstportrait mit Reich und Riley (und Chopin ist auch dabei)*. It refers to the American Minimalist composers Steve Reich and Terry Riley, whose music Ligeti first heard while he was in residence at Stanford University in 1972.[13] In *Selbstportrait,* Ligeti used an idea that was very popular with Minimalist composers in the late 1960s and early 1970s. The composer specifies a certain pattern of notes, usually with strict rhythm and a specific metronomic marking, and indicates an approximate number of repetitions. The difference between *Selbstportrait* and many other Minimalist compositions is that Ligeti is more specific in his indications. In *Selbstportrait* he instructs the performers to count the repetitions strictly up to eight; from eight to twelve a deviation of one repetition more or less is of no concern; from twelve to eighteen one to two more or less is acceptable; and past eighteen

---

[13]Jane Piper Clendinning, "The Pattern-Meccanico Compositions of György Ligeti," *Perspectives of New Music* 31/1 (Winter 1993), 222.

the number of repetitions is purely approximate.[14] Subtle changes
in the texture are brought about by slightly changing the patterns.

Ligeti combined the ideas of Riley (indeterminate repetitions)
and Reich (slow rate of pattern change) with his own musical
language to create a new type of composition, which Jane Piper
Clendinning calls a pattern-meccanico composition. Clendinning
has defined this as: a composition containing "several overlaid
linear strands, each of which is constructed from small groups of
pitches rapidly repeated in a mechanical fashion with gradual
changes of pitch content."[15] A precursor to this type of composition
is the seventh movement of *Musica Ricercata*. This is the first
example of indeterminacy in Ligeti's music. As in *Selbstportrait*, it is
very controlled indeterminacy, with everything being specified
except for the exact lining up of the two parts (exs. 4 and 5).

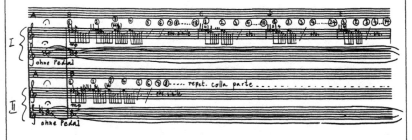

Ex. 4. *Selbstportrait*, beginning

---

[14]Prefatory notes to *Monument, Selbstportrait, Bewegung*
(Mainz: B. Schotts Söhne, 1976).
[15]Clendinning, 194-95.

9

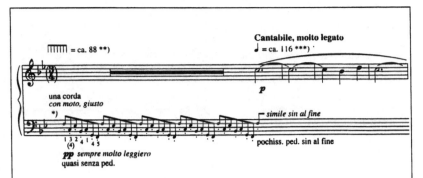

Ex. 5. *Musica Ricercata*, VII, beginning

Selbstportrait is also important because it is in this piece that
Ligeti first used the technique of blocked keys. At the beginning, the
left hand (of both pianists) silently holds down a chord, while the
right hand (of both) plays a pattern that runs across the notes in the
left hand (ex. 4). This produces holes in the pattern where the right
hand tries to play a note which is already depressed by the left hand.
These broken patterns are reminiscent of the African xylophone
music that would preoccupy Ligeti from the 1980s to the present.
"Touches bloquées" (Blocked Keys), the third étude, uses the same
technique. In this piece, the left hand silently holds down a chord
while the right hand weaves in and out with a fast scalar passage.
The importance of *Selbstportrait* to Ligeti's development can hardly
be overemphasized. Ligeti himself has stated that it was a "further
development of the pattern-illusion experiments of *Continuum for
Harpsichord* and the first step towards the piano études."[16]

---

[16]György Ligeti, notes to *György Ligeti: Keyboard Works*
(György Ligeti Edition 6, 1997), CD, Sony Classical SK 62307, 18.

10

Bewegung, the third of the three pieces for two pianos, uses the technique of superimposing the same melodic material at different tempi. The basic melodic material in *Bewegung* is scalar, which Ligeti expands, contracts, transposes, and inverts. "Cordes vides" (Open Strings), the second étude, also develops the idea of simultaneous different tempi, but uses perfect fifths as melodic material. The last page of *Bewegung* is also quite similar to the idea on which the later piano étude "Fanfares" is based. A continuous stream of fast notes contrasts with a slower group of chords in both pieces.

Monument, Selbstportrait, and *Bewegung* show Ligeti's growing concern with the manipulation of rhythm. In each piece he adopted a different approach in order to fully explore this idea. In *Monument,* he used grids, which gradually shift to create a myriad of rhythmic combinations, resulting in a composite sound present in neither part alone. *Selbstportrait* explores the possibilities of pattern composition, which can combine in somewhat unforeseen ways to also produce an illusory composite sound. In *Bewegung,* Ligeti applies contrapuntal devices to rhythm, and superimposes the same material at different speeds, also creating an illusory effect of speeding up and slowing down.

Ligeti develops all of these techniques even further in the *Études pour piano—premier livre,* which were composed in 1985. In 1980, Ligeti first heard the music of the American composer Conlon Nancarrow.[17] Evidently it made a lasting impression, for

---

[17]Steinitz, "Dynamics," 7.

11

Ligeti says that, to him, "the music for player piano by Conlon Nancarrow is the best music of any living composer today."[18] In 1982, Ligeti first encountered the recordings and writings of the ethnomusicologist Simha Arom, which acquainted him with the music of sub-Saharan Africa.[19] These two influences, combined with his interest in the recent developments of scientific thinking, have pushed Ligeti into his current style of rhythmic composition.

However, Ligeti's music also contains a very individual melodic and harmonic element. Much of his early music contains some type of chromatic wedge, with the most pure example being the subject of his *Invention*. The *Invention* was composed as an assignment for Veress. After thorough study of Bach's inventions, Ligeti was instructed to compose a "half-Bach" invention in his own style.[20] The subject of this invention is a chromatic wedge that originates on F, answered by the second voice an octave lower, with retrograde rhythm (ex. 6).

Ex. 6. *Invention,* beginning

---

[18]Quoted in Matthew Greenall, "Excellent Adventure," *Music Teacher* 76/1 (January 1997), 23.
[19]Steinitz, "Dynamics," 7.
[20]Ligeti, *Keyboard,* 10.

12

Capriccio No. 1 and *Capriccio No. 2* also have wedge-type figures, albeit not as symmetrical as the subject of the *Invention*. In *Capriccio No. 1*, Ligeti uses a certain type of chromatic figure which surrounds a single unplayed note (ex. 7). This note is almost always surrounded by at least three or four chromatic notes above and below. The wedge figures in *Capriccio No. 2* are even less symmetrical, but still retain the overall shape of a wedge with the exception of the last sonority (ex. 8). Also note the sonority that is repeated, at different transpositions, at the end of the first B section (ex. 9). This trichord, composed of a minor second and a minor third, is the "cluster with a gap" figure which signals closure in many of his later works.[21]

Ex. 7. *Capriccio No. 1*, m.17

Ex. 8. *Capriccio No. 2*, m.4

Ex. 9. *Capriccio No. 2*, m.60

---

[21]Bauer, 1151.

13

The subject of the fugal final movement of *Musica Ricercata* is also a chromatic wedge (ex. 10). This subject, derived from a "Ricercar cromatico" in Girolamo Frescobaldi's *Messa degli apostoli,* is an early example of the falling lament motive that is found in much of Ligeti's later music.[22] Perhaps the most obvious example of this lament figure, which is based on the funeral laments of the women of Siebenbürgen,[23] is in the sixth and final étude of the first book, "Automne à Varsovie" (Autumn in Warsaw). It is dedicated to his Polish friends, perhaps in recognition of the growing unrest in Poland in the early 1980s.[24] The melodic material is comprised almost entirely of descending chromatic scales. The descending patterns are constantly undergoing reduction, expansion, rhythmic diminution, rhythmic augmentation, until finally they run off the bottom of the keyboard at the end of the piece.

Ex. 10. *Musica Ricercata,* XI, beginning

---

[22]Richard Steinitz, "Weeping and Wailing," *Musical Times* 137/1842 (August 1996), 20.

[23]Jeffery Bossin, "György Ligeti's New Lyricism and the Aesthetic of Currentness: The Berlin Festival's Retrospective of the Composer's Career," *Current Musicology* 37/38 (1984), 237.

[24]Steinitz, "Dynamics," 13.

14

The fifth étude, "Arc-en-ciel" (Rainbow), has been described by Ligeti as "almost a jazz piece."[25] It is definitely the most lyrical of the set, and the least chaotic. However, still present are the combination of different tempi and the separation of the two hands into distinct units. The latter is most apparent in the tempo indications, with the right hand marked: Andante molto rubato, con eleganza, with swing; and the left hand marked: dolce, con tenerezza, sempre legato, molto espressivo.

The first book of études represents a culmination of many of Ligeti's prior experiments in rhythm and form. The *Konzert für Klavier und Orchester (Piano Concerto)*, written in 1985-88, is a sort of musical companion to the first book of études. The first three movements were composed in 1985, at the same time the études were composed. After hearing the premiere of those three movements, Ligeti decided that the piece sounded incomplete, so he composed two more movements, and the five-movement concerto was premiered in 1988.

The first movement is closely related to "Désordre," with a similar juxtaposition of shifting tonalities. The second movement is a complex canon, which again uses the descending chromatic lament figure.[26] The third movement is another example of a pattern-meccanico piece, with the orchestra playing at multiple

[25]Ligeti, *Works for Piano*, 11.
[26]Bossin, 237.

tempi at almost all times. The fourth movement is the second piece that Ligeti has based on a mathematical concept, in this case, fractals.[27] The fifth movement also uses multiple simultaneous tempi to create incredibly dense polyrhythms.

Both the *Piano Concerto* and the first book of études display Ligeti's continuing fascination with the manipulation of rhythm. He has managed to connect this desire to every aspect of composition. His early interest in counterpoint and polyphony has led him to apply these concepts not only to melody but also to rhythm.[28] His interest especially in the passacaglia form dates from his student days in Budapest, and the discovery that he could apply this to rhythm has led to an astounding explosion of rhythmic complexity in his music.[29]

Ligeti's "parallel interests in the folk musics of the world and developments in recent scientific thinking" have had an equally profound effect on his music.[30] He has said that his "concept of many-layered polyphony is influenced by [the] preoccupation with geometry, especially fractal geometry and the science of dynamical systems and deterministic chaos."[31] Ligeti has found in

---

[27]Steinitz, "Weeping," 22.
[28]Warnaby, 152.
[29]Steinitz, "Weeping," 18.
[30]Greenall, 23.
[31]From Ligeti's program note for the premiere of the first version of the *Violin Concerto* in September 1990; quoted in Steinitz, "Dynamics," 7.

modern science a concrete example of what he has always been trying to achieve in music.

To emphasize the fact that his compositional methods have remained largely the same, while the means and inspirations have changed, I refer to a study that identified four types of harmony which are present in Ligeti's recent music. These four types are:

1. Triads, major or minor in first inversion
2. 'Open fifth fields,' though not always arranged vertically in fifths
3. [0,1,6], which combines tritones, major sevenths, and fifths—also elaborations of this set such as [0,1,2,7] or [0,1,3,6,7] or a major triad with an added #fourth (raised fourth scale degree)
4. Seventh chords—usually major, minor, diminished or half-diminished in root position or inversion[32]

These harmonies are by no means restricted to Ligeti's late works. Triads occur in *Musica Ricercata* (ex. 11), and the triad with an added raised fourth is used in *Capriccio No. 1* (ex. 12). The set [0,1,6] appears throughout *Capriccio No. 2,* as do many types of seventh chords.

Ligeti has finally succeeded, with the combination of Balkan-style rhythms and lamento motifs, in "realizing the urge to

---

[32]S. Taylor, *The Lamento Motif: Metamorphosis in Ligeti's Late Style,* D.M.A. Dissertation (Cornell University, 1994), 75; quoted in Searby, 11.

17

Ex. 11. *Musica Ricercata*, III, m.22

Ex. 12. *Capriccio No. 1*, m.11

reconcile the avant-garde with the heritage of Bartók, as he had hoped to do during the early years in Budapest."[33] He accomplished this by becoming totally familiar with the avant-garde without being totally committed to it. When he first arrived in Vienna in 1956, he analyzed a great deal of serial music, but he realized a serious flaw in total serialism. He pointed out that, by nature, serialism was bound to destroy itself by reducing all music to a uniform entity, without color, shape, or expression.[34] Ligeti has come to use multi-serialism as a "well-balanced ordering of musical elements, not as a rigid compositional method."[35]

---

[33]Bossin, 239.

[34]György Ligeti, "Metamorphosis of Musical Form," *Die Reihe* 7 (1965), 10.

[35]Sean Rourke, "Ligeti's Early Years in the West," *Musical Times* 130/1759 (September 1989), 534.

18

Ligeti's music has gone through drastic changes due to his constantly changing interests, yet every piece is instantly recognizable because of the strength of his musical vision. As other composers continue the recent trend of rehashing nineteenth-century forms and harmonies, Ligeti is "trying to develop a harmony and melody which are no genuine return to tonality, which are neither tonal nor atonal but rather something else, above all in connection with a very high degree of rhythmic and metric complexity."[36] This is the impetus behind the études and the *Piano Concerto*. Perhaps, subconsciously, this has been the impetus behind all of his music. As Ligeti says: "To sum up the stylistic changes my music has gone through, first of all I should say that whenever I feel that certain melodic or rhythmic models or formal structures have gone stale, I switch my interest to some other area, but my basic approach remains unchanged."[37]

---

[36]Ligeti, quoted in Bossin, 238.

[37]*György Ligeti in Conversation with Peter Varnai, Josef Häusler, Claude Samuel, and Himself,* trans. Gábor J. Schabert (London: Eulenberg Books, 1983), 31-32.

19

Bibliography

Scores

Ligeti, György. *Capriccio Nr. 1 (1947); Invention (1948); Capriccio Nr. 2 (1947) für Klavier.* Mainz: B. Schotts Söhne, 1991.

———. *Études pour piano—premier livre.* Mainz: B. Schotts Söhne, 1986.

———. *Monument, Selbstportrait, Bewegung.* Mainz: B. Schotts Söhne, 1976.

———. *Musica Ricercata.* Mainz: Schott Musik International, 1995.

———. *Konzert für Klavier und Orchester.* Mainz: B. Schotts Söhne, 1990? [c1986].

Recordings

Ligeti, György. *Works for Piano.* Pierre Laurent-Aimard, piano. György Ligeti Edition 3. Sony Classical SK 62308, 1996. CD.

———. *Keyboard Works.* Irina Kataeva and Pierre Laurent-Aimard, piano. György Ligeti Edition 6. Sony Classical SK 62307, 1997. CD.

———. *Boulez Conducts Ligeti.* Ensemble Intercontemporain. Concertos for Piano, Cello, and Violin. Deutsche Grammophon 439 808-2, 1994. CD.

Books

György Ligeti in Conversation with Peter Varnai, Josef Häusler, Claude Samuel, and Himself. Translated by Gábor J. Schabert. London: Eulenberg Books, 1983.

20

Homer, Paul. "György Ligeti." *Contemporary Composers.* Edited
by Pamela Collins and Brian Morton. Chicago: St. James Press,
1992. 557.

Lichtenfeld, Monika. "György Ligeti." *Dictionary of Contemporary
Music.* Edited by John Vinton. New York: Dutton, 1974. 425-26.

Richart, Robert W. *György Ligeti: A Bio-Bibliography.* New York:
Greenwood Press, 1990.

Articles

Alues, Luminita. "Visible and Audibles Structures: Spatio-Temporal
Compromise in Ligeti's 'Magyar Etüdök.'" *Tempo* 183
(December 1992): 7-8.

Bauer, Amy. "György Ligeti. Capriccio Nr. 1 (1947); Invention
(1948); Capriccio Nr. 2 (1947) für Klavier." *Notes* 51/3 (March
1995): 1150-51.

Bodman, Christopher. "Darmstadt International Summer Course
for New Music 1976." *Composer* 59 (Winter 1976/77): 31.

Bossin, Jeffery. "György Ligeti's New Lyricism and the Aesthetic of
Currentness: The Berlin Festival's Retrospective of the
Composer's Career." *Current Musicology* 37/38 (1984): 233-39.

Clendinning, Jane Piper. "György Ligeti. Konzert für Klavier und
Orchester." *Notes* 48/4 (June 1992): 1453-55.

——. "The Pattern-Meccanico Compositions of György Ligeti."
Perspectives of New Music 31/1 (Winter 1993): 193-234.

Greenall, Matthew. "Excellent Adventure." *Music Teacher* 76/1
(January 1, 1997): 22-23.

21

Hicks, Michael. "Interval and Form in Ligeti's *Continuum* and *Coulée.*" *Perspectives of New Music* 31/1 (Winter 1993): 173-190.

Keller, Hans. "The Contemporary Problem." *Tempo* 89 (Summer 1969): 25-28.

Ligeti, György. "Metamorphosis of Musical Form." *Die Reihe* 7 (1965): 5-19.

——. "States, Events, Transformations." *Perspectives of New Music* 31/1 (Winter 1993): 165-70.

Nordwall, Ove. "György Ligeti." *Tempo* 88 (Spring 1969): 22-25.

Rourke, Sean. "Ligeti's Early Years in the West." *Musical Times* 130/1759 (September 1989): 532-35.

Searby, Mike. "Ligeti the Postmodernist?" *Tempo* 199 (January 1, 1997): 9-14.

Soria, Dorle J. "György Ligeti: Distinguished and Unpredictable." *Musical America* 107/4 (September 1987): 12-15, 27.

Steinitz, Richard. "Music, Maths, and Chaos." *Musical Times* 137/1837 (March 1996): 14-20.

——. "The Dynamics of Disorder." *Musical Times* 137/1839 (May 1996): 7-14.

——. "Weeping and Wailing." *Musical Times* 137/1842 (August 1996): 17-22.

Svard, Lois. "György Ligeti. Etudes pour piano." *Notes* 44/3 (March 1988): 578-79.

Thomas, Gavin. "New Times: New Clocks." *Musical Times* 134/1805 (July 1993): 376-79.

Warnaby, John. "Ligeti at 70." *Musical Opinion* 116 (May 1993): 152.

COMMENTARY ON THE STUDENT PAPER

Mr. Sullivan's purpose in this paper is to examine the available solo piano works of the Hungarian composer György Ligeti and to try to reach some general conclusions about them: what is noteworthy about Ligeti's piano style, how it has developed over time, and what particular features characterize Ligeti's piano writing and compositional approach. In order to achieve this goal, he has assembled a substantial bibliography of scores, recordings, articles, and books. The articles range from those in scholarly journals to reviews and criticism and a shorter piece in a magazine for teachers. A literature search this broad will invariably yield many helpful sources from a variety of perspectives.

Three introductory paragraphs summarize Ligeti's career and outline his early biography. The narrative then identifies, in chronological order, the piano works to be covered, explaining the salient musical features of each, which are illustrated in the musical examples. Note that the author has chosen not to present the entire chronological and style discussions separately, but rather to explain what is important about each piece as it is (chronologically) introduced. This is an effective strategy in a paper of this length; it enables the author to build directly on what came before without having to refer to a previous chronological discussion. The reader then understands how each new musical preoccupation contributed to the development of Ligeti's style (complex rhythms, pages 4–7; overlaying grids, pages 7–8; post-minimalism, pages 8–11; etc.).

Because the author introduces Ligeti's compositional interests one by one, the reader is able to see the composer's late style as both culmination and synthesis of the developments that had previously taken place (see pages 16–19). As Ligeti's modernist interests (serialism, mathematical approaches to rhythm) intermingled with traditional elements (folk musics, counterpoint, Bartókian Hungarianism), a unique compositional language emerged. Investigating this language was the author's main point; because of the clarity of presentation, the reader has no difficulty understanding how and from which influences the language developed.

One minor point should have been corrected. In the bibliography, the two dictionary articles listed under "Books" belong in the "Articles" section. A few statements in the paper, such as those pertaining to the composer's early biography, might have benefited from citation, rather than being allowed to stand as "common knowledge," even though they became common knowledge to the author in the research process. But such points are relatively minor, and they are easily remedied in the next writing project. Far more important is that, to reach his goal, the author had to synthesize a great deal of information from disparate sources, organize it and present it in an appropriate narrative style, draw his own conclusions, and cast the whole in a coherent form, all this in addition to coping with such mechanical matters as musical examples and citation form. The resultant paper is a fine piece of undergraduate research.

8

Style in Writing

"I quite agree with you," said the Duchess; "and the moral of that is—'Be what you would seem to be'—or if you'd like it put more simply—'Never imagine yourself not to be otherwise than what it might appear to others that what you were or might have been was not otherwise than what you had been would have appeared to them to be otherwise.'"

"I think I should understand that better," Alice said very politely, "if I had it written down."
—LEWIS CARROLL, ALICE IN WONDERLAND

THE MEANING OF "STYLE"

Style in writing consists of those aspects that make each author's writing individual. When, as a reader, you sense that an author is heavy-handed, elegant, terse, or bland, you are thinking about matters of style. Style encompasses vocabulary choices (for example, "pleased" vs. "ecstatic"), syntax (sentence structure, complexity, and length), and even the general musicality of the prose. Through style choices, the author projects a certain mood and affect (in addition to communicating information), thereby telling us something about himself or herself.

A comparison of two passages about the same piece, Chopin's nocturne for piano in B major, op. 62/1, will point up clear differences in style. The first example, written at the end of the nineteenth century, is by James Huneker.

[The B major nocturne] is faint with a sick, rich odor. The climbing trellis of notes, that so unexpectedly leads to the tonic, is charming and the chief tune has charm, a fruity charm. It is highly ornate, its harmonies dense, the entire surface overrun with wild ornamentation and a profusion of trills. The piece—the third of its sort in B—is not easy. . . .

Although this nocturne is luxuriant in style, it deserves warmer praise than is accorded it. Irregular as its outline is, its troubled lyrism is appealing, is melting, and the A-flat portion, with its hesitating, timid accents, has great power of attraction.[1]

The second example, from 1996, is by Jim Samson.

Throughout this opening section and the middle section Chopin exercises the greatest possible restraint in the ornamentation of his basic material. It is all the more magical, then, when the reprise of the main theme is presented entirely in trilled notes and allowed to open out, albeit briefly, into ecstatic, yet carefully controlled *fioriture*. Precisely because of the earlier simplicity of presentation, this reprise emerges as one of the supreme achievements of Chopin's ornamental melody. And characteristically it is halted in its tracks, interrupted by new sequential material, clearly derived from the opening section (the later stages), but essentially different from it and itself supplanted by a restatement of the semiquaver motive, now elaborated into the extended, curiously disembodied tracery which forms a coda to the nocturne. The overall shape of the piece transparently derives from a large-scale ternary design, but the detailed sequence of events—incorporating what we might describe as Chopin's strategies of formal concealment—is entirely unpredictable.[2]

These passages are intended for very different readers. In the first excerpt, Huneker (a pianist, music editor, and journalist) writes for his contemporaries, the music and art enthusiasts of a century ago, when such phrases as "faint with a sick, rich odor," "climbing trellis of notes," "fruity charm," and "troubled lyrism" would be evocative and meaningful, well within stylistic norms. Today, these phrases seem obscure and quaintly overwritten. Although some of the sentences are long, they are

---

[1]James Huneker, *Chopin: The Man and His Music* [1900] (New York: Dover, 1966), 149.

[2]Jim Samson, *Chopin* (New York: Schirmer, 1997), 264.

easy to follow. Huneker's tone is charmingly conversational, but he is also willing to suggest—when he says that the nocturne "deserves warmer praise than is accorded it"—that he is not afraid to offer an unconventional opinion. The writing seems to target not an academic audience but, rather, well-educated amateur pianists who could immediately play through the nocturne, and who had the leisure to do so.

By contrast, the second passage is thoroughly academic, as can be seen in its lengthy, multiclause sentences, its vocabulary (*"fioriture,"* "large-scale ternary design," "strategies of formal concealment"), and the author's interest in large- and small-scale formal procedures (contrasting Huneker's comments about the musical surface). The author is a professor, one of the world's most prominent authorities on Chopin, and his idiom reflects his habit of addressing academic audiences. As was stated earlier, academic thought merits academic style. What constitutes academic style, however, and when and how to use it, are questions that merit attention. It is not simply a matter of longer sentences for academics vs. shorter sentences for civilians, so to speak, nor is it a matter of twenty-dollar vocabulary vs. one-syllable, two-for-a-quarter words. Rather, it is a matter of the kind of thought an academic audience can be expected to share, and the kind of writing that reflects that thought process.

ACADEMIC STYLE TRAITS

Complex Sentence Structure

Academic style, unfortunately, has acquired negative associations: using many syllables and words rather than few; choosing to phrase a statement as the inverse of a negative rather than a simple positive ("it is not unlikely that Josquin des Prez studied with Johannes Ockeghem" or "the stirring sound of the Scottish bagpipes is not without a certain rude beauty"); using an obscure word or one from a foreign language when a commonplace English word would do as well or better; and relying upon mystifyingly complex sentence structure. True, these characteristics can make for difficult reading, yet they can also be necessary. Does Samson's excerpt illustrate some of them? Let's look again at a single sentence:

> And characteristically it is halted in its tracks, interrupted by new sequential material, clearly derived from the opening section (the later

stages), but essentially different from it and itself supplanted by a re-statement of the semiquaver motive, now elaborated into the extended, curiously disembodied tracery which forms a coda to the nocturne.

This sentence is, by any standard, huge and complex, and it is British rather than American; American readers will note the Britishisms of starting sentences with "and" and using "semiquaver" for "sixteenth-note." Samson chooses not to divide the sentence into smaller units, but this decision acknowledges that, even with all the component phrases, he is talking about *one thing:* the material that interrupts the return of the primary thematic material in the third major section of the piece. He explains the derivation of this "new" material, addressing both where in the work the passage originated and how it differs from that earlier material, and he finishes the sentence by describing the closing material of the work. All this is put in one sentence because every sentence is a complete unit, to be taken as a whole, and the complexity of his discussion of this musical interruption requires a single long sentence that commands the reader's focused concentration, not two or three short, humdrum statements. This is the essence of academic writing: intellectual and conceptual breadth of ideas requires a breadth and variety of syntactical structures to reflect it. Academic writing certainly carries some risk: at their worst, long and complex sentences do not hold together. That is, however, a fault of execution, not an intrinsic weakness of long sentences and academic writing per se.

Obscure Words

Here is another sentence from the Samson excerpt:

It is all the more magical, then, when the reprise of the main theme is presented entirely in trilled notes and allowed to open out, albeit briefly, into ecstatic, yet carefully controlled *fioriture.*

Surely, we wonder, there must be an English word equivalent to *fioriture?* In fact, there is not. *Fioriture* is an Italian word, the plural of *fiorit-ura* (literally, "flowering"), that has long been used to describe the orna-mental passages with which Italian opera singers from the seventeenth century on decorated their arias. Because the nocturne style (and partic-ularly the ornamental vocabulary) of Chopin and John Field was based in many ways on contemporary Italian opera singing, *fioriture* is precisely the word needed. Considerations such as these expand academic and musical vocabularies to include many words, both English and foreign, not often seen in other kinds of writing.

First Person Plural

One of the (now less common) formulas of academic writing consists of using the corporate first person plural, the so-called "papal we" or "royal we." In most cases, this is an affectation, a bald-faced pretense of objectivity when a subjective opinion is being offered. The difference this single word makes can be great. Compare the differing tone in the following two sentences:

> I tend to view big band jazz as a hybrid popular form.

> We tend to view big band jazz as a hybrid popular form.

The first sentence is a statement of individual opinion, no more threatening than any other, to be evaluated on its merits. This version proclaims, in its use of the first person singular, that it is an opinion, which means that the author is actively taking responsibility for it. The first person plural of the second sentence, though, implies some kind of consensus of the well-informed and authoritative, and in doing so it allows the author to hide behind this imagined consensus, taking little or no responsibility for the opinion and maintaining a kind of false modesty. The reader who appreciates big band jazz, suddenly made uneasy by this kind of wording, might begin to wonder if "hybrid" signifies impurity more than cross-fertilization, if "popular" implies ephemeral more than widely appreciated. In fact, the second sentence is the same statement of opinion the first was, the only addition being pomposity.

There are times when first person plural implies a teaching context, and in these cases it ought to be kept and maintained. One might say, "we see, in example 2, a conscious use of archaic harmony," and it ought to be literally true: teacher (the author) and students (the readers) all see the harmony in question. "We now understand this to mean . . ." would simply be an extension of this idea; the teaching and explanation having taken place, author and readers now share an understanding and are on the same wavelength, thus "we." But the dividing line between "we understand" (following a clear explanation) and "we view" (which is perhaps just an ex cathedra statement of opinion or preference) can be very thin. In general, because of the negative effect first person plural can have on tone, it should be used with great care.

Passive Voice

Overuse of the passive voice is a common flaw in novice academic writing. Passive voice renders the object of an action, or the effect of a verb, into the subject of a sentence. That is: for the active construction "we made mistakes," where the subject of the sentence, *we,* is the agent or cause of the action, passive voice would have "mistakes were made by us," or (worse) "mistakes were made." In this second example of a passive sentence, notice that the original subject—the doer of the action—has completely disappeared. The action takes place in an eerie, unpopulated world where things happen without cause and responsibility for actions belongs elsewhere. Now compare the following passages:

Active voice

The development section makes extensive use of counterpoint, which propels the unstable harmony to several distant keys. This harmonic exploration reaches the dominant of the submediant ($V/_{vi}$) at bar 70, and from that point a gradual decrescendo and thinning of texture lead gently back to both the tonic and recapitulation at bar 76.

Passive voice

In the development, counterpoint is used extensively, and the unstable harmony is propelled to several distant keys. The dominant of the submediant ($V/_{vi}$) is reached at bar 70, and (after a gradual decrescendo and thinning of texture) the tonic and recapitulation are reached at bar 76.

The second version is far less dynamic, and it implies that the musical events described occur in that bland universe where "mistakes were made." The sheer sameness—"is used," "is propelled," "is reached," "are reached"—tires the reader and implies that this laborious, blow-by-blow description of compositional events amounts to little of importance. The first version, though, supplies an agent for every action, and a sense of continuity results. We see the passage in terms of compositional choices and musical effects, which suggests a forward-moving musical narrative unfolding in real time.

Passive voice is not necessarily wrong, however. This excerpt from the Samson passage

> It is all the more magical, then, when the reprise of the main theme is presented in trilled notes

is better stated in passive than active voice. It appears in the course of a discussion of musical events, and we *know* that the composer is responsible for all those musical events anyway. To say

> it is all the more magical, then, when the composer presents the reprise of the main theme in trilled notes

would seem an unwarranted intrusion: we were discussing musical events, not the composer's invisible hand. But in this case the passive voice is used *once;* it does not appear often enough to anaesthetize the reader, and there is no doubt about who is responsible for the event.

Traditional Academic Organization

Term papers, master's theses, doctoral dissertations, and scholarly articles often follow a particular plan of organization. With the laudable goal of clarity, this format dictates that the writer begin with a brief statement of its contents, in the form of a fleshed-out outline, and that this same material also appear throughout the body of the paper and in the conclusion. For example, an introduction might state:

> First, I will identify several examples of this type of monophonic
> writing in nineteenth-century American music. Next, it will be
> demonstrated that its origins lie in the work-chants of the colonial
> slaves in the New World. Finally, the significance of this music to
> both monodic performance practices and Colonial Studies in
> general will be evaluated.

This passage would benefit from more active voice and substantial editing. For example: "Examples of this kind of monophony are found in nineteenth-century American music, and its origins lie in the work-chants of the colonial slaves, making the music significant both for monodic performance practices and Colonial Studies." But even if this

passage were to remain three sentences in length, it might be a workable beginning, particularly if the uses of passive voice were amended.
In terms of content, though, it is really more outline than true prose
paragraph, in that the sentences don't follow naturally one from the
other, for they shadow a narrative that would take much longer than
three sentences. When an outline serves as beginning, authors tend to
keep touching base with it in the course of the paper. In such cases, the
difference between informing the reader where in the process he or
she is—a good idea—and merely reiterating the outline is easily
missed.

Consider the second sentence of this introduction: "Next, it will be
demonstrated that its origins lie in the work-chants of the colonial slaves
in the New World." In the body of the paper, this point might reappear
in several ways. After the examples have been identified, as the section
on origins is about to begin:

> We will see that the source musics of this American monophony
>
> are to be found in colonial work-chants.

After the origins, and immediately before the music's significance for
monodic performance and Colonial Studies is discussed:

> As has been shown, the work-chants of the colonial slaves
>
> provided the source material for these surviving examples of
>
> American monophonic writing.

Finally, as part of the conclusions:

> Colonial work-chants, as has been demonstrated, were the point of
>
> origin of this kind of uniquely American solo song.

Clearly, the author has not adequately developed the point (although
it may be developed elsewhere), he or she is merely repeating it, and the
effect is leaden. It is a good idea, whenever recapitulating a thought or
touching base with the broader structure, to *make sure there is something
new in the sentence,* either an elaboration of the idea or a clear transition
to another point. The author reminds the reader where he or she is, while

at the same time moving forward and doing something that was not previously done. Two examples:

> We will now see that the source musics of this American
> monophony are to be found in colonial work-chants, particularly
> the chants of the native workers most closely involved with the
> colonials' domestic lives.

> While we can see that colonial work-chants were in some sense the
> point of origin of this uniquely American kind of solo song, the
> transformation of this music was so radical that the practical idea of
> "origin" has to be reexamined.

Continuity and momentum require that no sentence duplicate another, even for the good purpose of clarifying organization. Rather than clarify, a sentence that duplicates tends to "show the seams" in the outline with no compensating benefit. Particularly in a multisection academic paper, the author cannot afford repeatedly to go over the same ground.

Another common feature of academic writing is the so-called literature review. Required in many theses and dissertations, this is a section (often a separate chapter) devoted exclusively to writings related to one's topic of interest, with brief summaries and critiques of each item. While in some cases a review of the literature provides helpful background, more often it results in a turgid, mechanically written passage that contributes little to the progess of the work. It is unnecessary, in most cases, to explain why previous scholarship has fallen short; better would be a separate annotated bibliography provided to the academic committee, with earlier sources being cited in the body of the work only as relevant. Authors will ultimately be the best judges of when such treatments of previous literature should be included.

Even the best and most vibrant academic writing cannot exist without parenthetical elaborations and explanations, citations and critiques of earlier work, advanced vocabulary, and other easily satirized characteristics. The key lies in the restrained use of such things, so that their effectiveness is not diminished. As in musical analysis, the challenge is to find a judicious balance between subtlety and what is easily comprehended.

FASHIONING CLEAR SENTENCES

"Less is more," a familiar saying, holds true in the formulation of sentences. While complex syntax can be a positive style trait, academic authors (student and professional alike) too often get lost in tangents and elaborations. Consider this sentence:

> The problems resulting from defining the formal content of
> Chopin's Ballades in terms of sonata form (or style, or process, or
> principle) only serve to complicate further the task of the critic,
> scholar, and performer, for while the Ballades share with sonata
> form certain analogous features (contrasting themes, contrasting
> key areas, development or expansion of thematic and motivic
> material), after thorough examination they may be seen to
> represent much less than the totality of the Ballade-narrative, and
> ultimately suggest that a wholly untraditional analytical approach is
> better suited to the task.

This 92-word sentence is not even particularly complex; it just appears that way because of all the asides. Too many words confuse rather than explain: the reader begins to lose sight of whether the subject of the sentence is the problems resulting from the original comparison, as first stated, or the Ballades themselves, or the analogous features in the two forms. Which of these necessitates a new approach? The primary culprit here is distance: so many words occur between "problems," "after thorough examination they," and "ultimately suggest" that the many stated plural items run together in the reader's mind: problems, Ballades, and analogous features.

Four principal ideas make up the sentence:

- the idea that there are problems resulting from a sonata-form approach to the Ballades, and that they complicate analysis
- what the similarities between the Ballades and sonata form are
- that these similarities do not account for enough of the works' content to support analysis in these terms
- the call for a new analytical approach

While it may not be necessary to devote a separate sentence to each idea, they are far too much for one; two well-ordered, severely pruned sentences would be far preferable.

Trimming is the first priority. To speak of "defining the formal content . . . in terms of sonata form" is repetitious; how else to define formal content except in terms of form? Rather, we *view* or *analyze* works in terms of a particular form. The first parenthesis is unnecessary; "sonata form" will do just fine, because this is not the place to debate whether "form" is the best way to describe one of the most commonly studied and identified compositional processes of the eighteenth and nineteenth centuries. The remaining parenthethical material, which explains the similarities between the Ballades and sonata form, needs to be brought closer to the first mention of the sonata idea and shortened.

We can recast the opening idea to explain the sonata-Ballade comparison with greater clarity. Since there will be a logical change of direction—that is, there are similarities but they will not prove definitive— let's begin with "although" ("while" would also work):

Although Chopin's Ballades have such typical sonata-form

characteristics as contrasting themes and key areas and thematic

development,

Rather than introducing other issues, it will be better to follow this single line of thought, namely where these similarities will or will not lead. To this end, we retrieve a line from later in the original sentence and end up with sufficient material for a shorter, clearer, statement:

Although Chopin's Ballades have such typical sonata-form

characteristics as contrasting themes and key areas and thematic

development, these aspects represent much less than the totality of

the Ballade-narrative.

The original sentence refers to the "task" of the critic, scholar, and performer. Which task is shared by these people? Rather than leave this vague task to the imagination of the reader, it would be better to save a few words and name it—say, analysis. The phrase "after thorough examination may be seen to represent" is unnecessary; we assume that the author has examined the works thoroughly, and we do not require reassurance. At the end, "wholly untraditional" may be replaced by "new," saving one word (but six syllables). The remaining ideas, that analysis is complicated rather than facilitated by sonata-Ballade linkage and that a new model is needed, make more sense combined than they do separated, as they are in the original version. An economical way of putting them might be:

> The sonata model thus causes more problems than it solves in the
> analysis of these pieces, and it seems clear that a new analytical
> approach is called for.

Together, these two sentences comprise 58 words, less than two-thirds the length of the original single sentence, and they present its ideas in a clearer, more elegant way. Elegance in writing—more a matter of simplicity and equilibrium than of linguistic curlicues—consists chiefly of a balance between three things: economy, the logical presentation of ideas, and an attractive variety in wording and syntax. But an overemphasis on economy results in curtness, an obsessive attention to logical presentation at the expense of other considerations can produce mechanical writing, and exaggerating an attractive variety makes for florid prose. Striving for the balance between these three qualities will eventually produce writing that is clear and enjoyable to read.

Taste

Elegance is also a matter of taste, and it is the responsibility of every author to exercise restraint in the choice of language and metaphor, and wisdom in the consideration of what readers will appreciate, or *not* appreciate, seeing in print. Here is a passage by Cuthbert Girdlestone on the finale of Mozart's piano concerto in B-flat major, K. 456:

> The second subject then displays its lopsided mass; it advances with
> the nimble haste of a cripple, one of whose crutches has been stolen,
> and who pursues the thief brandishing the other. The woodwinds mock
> it and, when it changes places and gives itself to the oboe and bassoon,
> the piano jeers at it too.[3]

To quote Chaucer's Pardoner, "what needeth it to sermone of it more?" Although Girdlestone strives for the common touch by calling up an image all readers might be able to imagine, it tells us almost nothing about the music it purportedly describes. The image is so grotesquely pa-

---

[3]Cuthbert Girdlestone, *Mozart and His Piano Concertos* [1948] (Norman, OK: University of Oklahoma Press, 1952), 274. Girdlestone is discussing the deployment of thematic material in the finale of Mozart's piano concerto K. 456 in B-flat.

thetic, moreover, that it negates any imagined benefits of stylistic liveliness or unpretentiousness. This sort of lapse of taste, authors may safely assume, will *never* carry with it enough compensating merit to be worthwhile.

An aside here: the use of the word "cripple" reminds us that older sources frequently use terminology and reflect worldviews that cannot be presented today without qualification. The direct quotation or even excerpting of such sources should not be restricted in an academic environment, but by the same token it should be done within the proper context, with explanation, judicious use of paraphrase, and so on. For example, racist passages by Richard Wagner or Daniel Gregory Mason (which I do *not* quote here) need not necessarily be quoted in all their ugly particulars, and when particulars are quoted, it is only appropriate to do so with a contextual explanation and with a specific goal in mind.

Transitions

Transitions are words and phrases that lead from one idea to another, relating the new idea to the idea preceding it in a particular way, guiding the reader through the author's line of thought. Examples of such relationships include *amplification* (for which one might use "furthermore," "moreover," or "in addition"), *contrast* or *qualification* ("but," "however," "on the other hand"), and *illustration* ("for example," "for instance," "take as an example"). Perhaps the second idea intensifies the first, perhaps it is a logical result of the first, perhaps it contrasts or contradicts the previous idea or stands apart from it in some way; the relationship of the two ideas will tell you which transitional word or phrase to use. "Moreover," for example, indicates that the writer will develop the point further. "On the other hand" indicates that the writer will go on to make a point somewhat contrary to what has just been said. These kinds of transistions, including "incidentally," "nonetheless," and "in conclusion," often make the difference between a passage that is clear and easy to follow and what seems to be a random succession of sentences.

Imagine a discussion of slow introductions to allegro movements, and the distinction between early uses of this device and a later, more famous piece that also used it and which everyone now assumes to have been first. In the course of such a discussion, one might see this paragraph:

> Beethoven's use of the slow introduction is a case in point. The first movement of his op. 13 piano sonata ("Pathétique") is often considered revolutionary in its use of this device, usually seen to this

point only in the opening movements of symphonies. The material from this introduction reappears two more times in the course of the movement, not just at the beginning. The Italian composer Muzio Clementi used a slow introduction in his piano sonata op. 34/2, composed two to three years before the "Pathétique." Clementi's introductory material provides the basis of the rest of the movement, which was not true of Beethoven's, and this material returns in more varied guises. Beethoven's movement is neither the first, nor the most adventurous, early use of the slow introduction.

This paragraph makes a kind of sense, but following it is difficult. There are too many jumps between ideas and little flow. Here is the same paragraph, with transitions added in brackets:

Beethoven's use of the slow introduction is a case in point. The first movement of his op. 13 piano sonata ("Pathétique") is often considered revolutionary in its use of this device, usually seen to this point only in the opening movements of symphonies. [Moreover,] The material from this introduction reappears two more times in the course of the movement, not just at the beginning. [But] The Italian composer Muzio Clementi used a slow introduction in his piano sonata op. 34/2, composed two to three years before the "Pathétique." [Significantly,] Clementi's introductory material provides the basis of the rest of the movement, which was not true of Beethoven's, and this material returns in more varied guises. [Therefore, despite its reputation] Beethoven's movement is neither the first, nor the most adventurous, early use of the slow introduction.

The transitions signal when an idea contrasts with what preceded it, when it turns a corner, or follows logically, or intensifies the previous idea. On a general level, they ensure a continuity of thought that would not have been apparent from the mere succession of ideas.

Variety

Variety is an aspect of writing in which a musical comparison is of great value. If we imagine a work with equal (say, four-bar) phrasing throughout, with no variation in textural or harmonic complexity or lyrical interest, we envision crushing boredom. Consider a prose equivalent:

> Music of the American Indians is of increasing interest today. Serious study of Native American musics is a relatively recent phenomenon. Some nineteenth-century composers sought to incorporate Indian elements in their compositions. The twentieth century saw a fully developed school of Indianist composition. The resulting works were *about* Indians rather than being in any way musically authentic. Most American listeners remained largely ignorant of true Native American music. Current research seeks to fill this gap in American musical understanding.

The succession of similarly constructed sentences numbs by its very sameness. Consider, instead:

> Music of the American Indians is of increasing interest today. Serious study of actual Native American musics is, however, a relatively recent phenomenon. While some nineteenth-century composers sought, tentatively, to incorporate Indian elements in their compositions, it wasn't until the twentieth century that a fully developed school of Indianist composition evolved. The resulting works were *about* Indians rather than being in any way musically authentic, and as a result most American listeners remained largely ignorant of true Native American music. One of the central goals of current research, then, is filling this gap in American musical understanding.

The passage is greatly improved simply by combining some sentences and adding transitions to others. In general, variety is the spice of lively writing: a lengthy sentence is often best followed by a simple and direct one, and next may come one with parallel construction, and all of them may be contrasted by a sentence with a parenthetical explanation or aside. The key is to follow no rule, but to avail oneself of all the variety the English language affords.

PUNCTUATION

The purpose of punctuation, in English or any other language, is to divide and separate thoughts so that they are most easily understood. Sometimes differences in punctuation result in differences in meaning:

> Musicians who are underpaid should strike.
>
> Musicians, who are underpaid, should strike.

The first sentence, which has no punctuation other than the final period, states that those musicians who are underpaid should strike. The second, which puts "who are underpaid" as a parenthetical phrase between two commas, says instead that *all* musicians are underpaid and that they all should strike. The first sentence identifies "musicians who are underpaid" as a subset of all musicians, and it is this group of musicians that is the subject of the sentence, while the second sentence uses "who are underpaid" as a parenthetical descriptor of *all* musicians, leaving "musicians" alone as the subject. The difference in meaning between the two sentences is substantial.

More often, though, punctuation does not change meaning this radically. It governs rhythm and flow—what is sometimes called the musical aspect of writing. Ideas are separated from each other by periods, commas, semicolons, colons, and dashes for clarification, much as we clarify our meaning when we speak with pauses of different lengths for breathing and dramatic effect. One good way to check punctuation is to read drafts of your writing aloud; if you misread a passage, the chances are good that the punctuation is at fault.

Colon, Semicolon, and Comma

The colon, semicolon, and comma are frequently confused, but each has specific uses. The *colon* temporarily stops a sentence and announces to the reader that a quotation, a list of items, an explanation, or an example will follow. (It is also used in numerical ratios and times of day.)

The essential dances of the Baroque suite include: Allemande, Courante, Sarabande, and Gigue.

The *semicolon* is a fairly lengthy pause that separates independent clauses (that is, clauses that can stand as complete sentences), as in this example:

Brahms had no need of learning the Hungarian-Gypsy style from Reményi; it had been popular for decades before their first meeting.

Semicolons also separate elements in a list, either when the list is inordinately long or when the elements require shorter pauses themselves. Here is an expanded version of the first example:

Traditional dances of the Baroque suite include: Allemande; Courante, or occasionally Corrente; Sarabande; Gigue, or occasionally Giga; and such optional movements as Gavotte, Bourée, and Air.

The *comma*, finally, is the punctuation mark that signifies the shortest pause, merely a figurative intake of breath. A pair of commas is often used to enclose a parenthetical or explanatory clause, and it is the commonest of errors to omit one comma or the other. In this context, they are best thought of as parentheses:

Eric Clapton's recordings, his blues background notwithstanding, embrace a wide variety of styles.

The dash (sometimes called the em dash, after the printer's measurement of its length) provides an interruptive pause and is often used for authorial asides. It is either written with two hyphens (without spaces before or after) or—if your computer program will do it, and most will— an actual dash.

In Bartók's music, time signatures that seem to be metrical anomalies—at least within the traditional Western repertoire—are in fact rooted in ancient Hungarian folk music.

Interpretations of bel canto opera are too often marred by fidelity to the score—fidelity that would have been unthinkable by the opera singers of the bel canto eras, who gained fame through the virtuosity of their ornamentation.

But be careful not to use too many dashes. An abundance of dashes can give your writing the sense of being punchy and overly emphatic, or (conversely) it can give the impression of directionlessness, suggesting that you cannot write without interrupting yourself.

Specifically Musical Uses of Punctuation

Certain conventions of punctuation are used in connection with generic titles of classical works, particularly where performance indications serve as section titles. The movement is usually separated from the performance or mood indication by a colon (Minuet: Andante). Performance indications are separated from each other by a semicolon (thus the first movement of a Haydn symphony could be designated Largo; Allegro), and movements are separated from each other, when they are not given separate lines in the program, by em dashes: Allegro—Adagio—Allegro.

With respect to titles in general, we distinguish between titles of complete works and sections within them through formatting and punctuation—italics (or, as a weak second choice, underlining) for complete works, and quotation marks for parts thereof. Thus, one of the songs in Robert Schumann's song cycle *Dichterliebe* is "Aus alten Märchen." Even though it is customary to italicize foreign words, when an entire foreign phrase appears within quotation marks it is generally not done because it looks too fussy.

ACCURACY IN WORDING

Nothing can ruin a piece of writing like the wrong word. One recent (and hilarious) error from a political magazine involved using the word *eschatological* (pertaining to the theological study of Last Things, such as death and final judgment) when *scatological* (pertaining to solid human bodily wastes) was meant. A more innocent example might be the common confusion of *mitigate* (to moderate, or make less severe) and *militate* (to have force or influence); one can militate against something, but one cannot mitigate against anything, despite how often that construction is seen.

Similar pitfalls are presented by the pairs *comprise* and *compose* and *imply* and *infer*, which sound similar but mean different things. For the first pair, the rule is best memorized: *the whole comprises the parts, and the parts compose the whole.* Thus, a Baroque dance suite comprises at least four different dance movements, but an Allemande, Courante, Sarabande, and Gigue compose (or make up, or constitute) the Baroque dance suite. With *imply* and *infer*, both words pertain to what is hinted or guessed at; the distinction has to do with who is responsible for the conclusions. *Imply* has to do with meaning or significance suggested by words or actions (that is, latent within the subject itself), while *infer* reflects assumptions made or conclusions drawn (i.e., made by someone outside the subject in question):

Milhaud's use of jazz in *La Création du monde* implies his awareness of its growing popularity.

We can infer, from Milhaud's use of jazz in *La Création du monde*, that he was aware of its growing popularity.

A comprehensive list of similar word-pairs and problematic terms would be impossibly long. (Consult Strunk and White, *The Elements of Style,* chapter 4, for more.) But authors must repeatedly be urged that *accuracy in wording is crucial.* Make sure that you are aware of both specific meaning *(denotation)*, and the implication *(connotation)* of the words you use. To say

The work was in a $\frac{3}{4}$ rhythm, and had the character of a waltz

is to commit an error of denotation, because $\frac{3}{4}$ time is a meter, not a rhythm. Rhythm and meter have very different meanings, although "rhythm" is often wrongly used for both. Saying

The composer drags the tempo in this phrase

when what is intended is

The composer directs that this phrase be played *ritardando* is an error of connotation, because "drags" is a negative word, suggesting laziness and heaviness, while *ritardando* explains that the tempo slows down.

Wording that is only superficially accurate is also best changed, such as in the sentence "In the closing section, the composer repeats the primary theme verbatim." It is true that one of the meanings of "verbatim" is "exactly," but the literal meaning comes from Latin, "word for word." To repeat a theme, or any group of musical notes, "word for word" is impossible. The error here is only partially one of denotation, since one of the meanings of the word is acceptable; rather, the word "verbatim" is simply an inelegant choice, much better corrected than allowed to stand.

Beat, Meter, Rhythm

The words beat, meter, and rhythm, all of which have to do with the measurement of musical time, are probably the most often confused words in the musical lexicon. *Beat* is simply a pulse, that which marks time in regular intervals. *Meter* is the regular organizing of beats, for example in repeating groups of three or four, and assigning at least one beat in each group (often the first) greater significance or emphasis. *Rhythm* is any sequence of durations, repeated or not. Dances, historically, have had characteristic rhythms associated with them, such as dotted eighth note-sixteenth note-eighth note for the siciliano:

Or dotted-quarter-eighth- quarter-quarter for a pavane:

That and *Which*

In American (as opposed to British) English there is a clear distinction between *that* and *which*. (This despite the common, somewhat lazy practice of using *which* in virtually all cases, which adds a slightly fussy and pretentious tone.) *That* is a restrictive pronoun; it distinguishes the item under discussion from like items. For example, "the cello that soars out over the rest of the ensemble" suggests one cello among several, or many, acting in a specific way. By contrast, *which* is nonrestrictive; it indicates that there is no further limitation on the indicated object. "The cello, which soars out over the rest of the ensemble" indicates that there is only one cello in the ensemble, and (for the moment at least) it enjoys a solo role. In cases of uncertainty, one convenient (if not *always* correct) method is to look for a parenthetical phrase within commas; *which* usually follows a comma, while *that* rarely does.

Accuracy in Spelling and Punctuation

There is nothing to be said here about spelling and punctuation other than *do it right!* Your computer's spell-checking software will not catch every error, particularly when homophones (e.g., *led* and *lead, past* and *passed, to* and *too*) are involved. Similarly, the fact that much of the American populace seems unaware of the difference between "it's" (the contraction of *it is*) and "its" (the possessive; something belonging to it) does not mean that such carelessness is somehow excusable in writing. Errors of this kind bespeak not only ignorance but slovenliness; it is as if the author is either unable or lazily disinclined to spell or punctuate accurately. In either case, this is a message no author can ever afford to send.

Aggregate Titles: Singular or Plural?

Musical works frequently have plural titles, such as *Piano Variations.* Such works are considered as wholes and therefore are singular. For example, it is correct to say "Brahms's *Variations on a Theme of Händel* has always been popular among pianists" (not "*have* always been popular") because this is a single work, even though it comprises many variations. By comparison, there would be no problem with saying "Brahms's variations *have* always been popular among pianists," because he wrote not only many variations but also several variation sets, and no specific set is designated here; the subject is unquestionably plural.

Awkward Wording

The final arbiter of good writing is not a style book or some other external authority, but rather—as suggested before—the reader's ear. Phrases that make the reader stumble, hesitate, or reread them must be changed, whether or not they are grammatically correct. As a general rule, a phrase or sentence that troubles you for any reason should be taken back to the workshop; a much better solution undoubtedly awaits.

Obvious infelicities include constructions such as "one such example appears in Example 3" or "the same figure appears in Figure 4." There is nothing actually wrong with what is being said, but the repetition of "example" and "figure" when the second uses have different meanings confounds the reader. Any coincidental repetition of a word, as opposed to repetition for rhetorical emphasis or clarity, merits close scrutiny and (likely) adjustment.

Try to detect awkwardness of any kind—wording, poor treatment of transitions, ambiguity of meaning—in the proofreading process. As these are subtler matters than spelling, punctuation, and subject-verb agreement, practice and experience will be the best guides in learning what to look for and how to rectify problematic passages. Cultivating a dependable "writer's ear," an instinctive sense of the rhythm and flow of the language, is a long-term (indeed, an unending) process. All authors, in addition to perfecting their own writing, must therefore read a great deal, assimilating as much as possible from the writing they find most effective.

TOWARD A PERSONAL STYLE

There is no more valuable advice on the subject of writing style than that of E. B. White: "To achieve style, begin by affecting none—that is, place yourself in the background."[4] The priority is your subject; strive to produce clear, communicative writing, not to make an impression. Similar advice has long been given to nervous musical performers: worry about the *music*, not how well or how poorly you're doing. Letting go of the ego in such a situation will, paradoxically, produce writing far more likely to reflect well upon its author (or performances of which the interpreter can be proud).

White also gave the payoff for this advice, in a timeless phrase: "No writer long remains incognito."[5] From diligent, intelligent work on writing, a unique voice inevitably results.

---

[4]William Strunk, Jr., and E. B. White, *The Elements of Style,* 3rd ed. (London: Macmillan, 1979), 70.

[5]Ibid., 67.

9

The Final Manuscript

*Do the little things well; then will come the great things begging to
be done.*

—CHINESE PROVERB

GENERAL FORMAT

The following suggestions are intended to produce a paper that is easy to
look at, read, and preserve. "Standard form," which all compilations of
style guidelines purport to follow, is in fact not nearly so standard as it
would be convenient to believe. The requirements of your instructor, college, university, or publication, should they differ from the advice and examples given here, take precedence.

1. Binding, Paper, Duplication. Papers must be stapled, paper-
clipped, bound in some way, or kept in an envelope (this last is most appropriate when submitting an article for publication). Ask if your instructor has a preference; do not overlook this matter and expect him or her to
keep track of a pile of loose pages. Worse yet is to leave the sheets unsep-
arated after they leave the printer. Make life easier for your reader, not
harder! Pages are to be printed on one side only, and paper quality is to
be good—not necessarily premium stationery, but not newsprint either.

2. Word Processing. Use a computer with word-processing software
such as Microsoft Word or WordPerfect (or any other you like; my intent

is to illustrate, not to advertise), and make sure your software has a foot-note function—cut-and-paste editing of academic work without such a function is nearly impossible. If you are a student who does not own a computer with such software, the computer lab at your college or univer-sity will certainly have it, and you will discover in the meantime that word-processing has countless other benefits. In fact, some people no longer accept papers typed on the traditional (but fast becoming archaic) typewriter. Except for truly exceptional cases, one should never turn in handwritten papers.

If you are not a student, and you do not have immediate access to a computer lab, simply remember that word-processed writing is standard in publishing and that the initial appearance of your paper or article will affect how well it is read and received. Many copy shops sell computer time, so even when you don't own a personal computer you can still write with one.

3. Copies. Always keep a photocopy or a second printed copy of your paper for yourself. Occasionally papers are lost (by student or professor), and a copy is the best safeguard against lost work. (Of course you will keep your computer disks, but disks are easily lost or damaged, and they sometimes decay to the point of unreadability.) If you are asked for a du-plicate copy, "I didn't bother to copy it and my computer crashed and I seem to have lost my disks when I changed apartments" is an insufficient excuse. A complete loss of work is a disaster that is easily avoided.

Corollary: Save All Notes and Drafts. Keep all notes and drafts so that you can easily verify a quotation, a wording, a citation; your instruc-tor (or another scholar) may need more background information than ap-pears in the final draft. Also save your notes on computer, and save the files in more than one place. All your research (not just a final paper draft) is a database, whether it consists of notes scrawled on notebook pa-per or a formal, annotated bibliography, and you never know when in life you will want to return to it—it may be during the grading process or twenty years later.

4. Title Page. Every paper should have a title page with this informa-tion: title of the paper, name of assignment if appropriate (e.g., "Opinion Paper"), course number and name of course, professor's name, and date. Number all pages. (Ask if your instructor has a preference for where the page number should appear; many prefer bottom center.) When submitting an article for publication, the title page should have the title of the paper, the author's name, and either the author's university/professional affiliation *or* city of residence. In an article or paper, pagination begins after the title page; in a book or book manuscript, pagination of the front matter (title page, publishing information, preface, and so on) is done in lower case roman numerals, and it begins with the first page on which printing appears. Pagination of the text itself begins with arabic numeral 1.

5. Spacing and Margins. Double-space your essay, and use margins of 1.5 inches all around. Where specific guidelines (such as university thesis formats that accommodate binding) contradict this, follow the specific guidelines. Pages with headings, such as the first pages of chapters, will need more space at the top. This arrangement of margins and spacing will provide relatively light text density, so the paper will be easy to read, with ample room for the instructor or editor to write comments.

6. Block Quotations. Set off a quotation of more than two lines with an extra carriage return before and after it, and by indenting an extra half-inch at both the left and right margins for the paragraph(s) of the quotation. (Most programs allow you, with a keystroke or two, to indent paragraphs.) The margins will now be wider than those of the rest of the paper, and the quotation will stand out from the text as a small "block." You do not need to change font or font size. Because you will cite the quotation in a footnote or endnotes, it will be followed by a small superscript number. Put citation numbers outside—that is, after—every punctuation mark except the dash. (More on citations below.)

7. Bibliography. Bibliographies are sometimes used for scholarly articles but never for concert reviews, program notes, and other less formal kinds of writing. (For classroom assignments, however, they are often required and are helpful for student and instructor alike.) Bibliographies will ideally account for all sources consulted, where further reading may be done. Since all these sources will probably not be found in the footnotes, a bibliography enables the author to include them. Formatting for footnotes and bibliographies differs with regard to punctuation and presentation, so examples of each will appear later in this chapter, in the section Sample Citations.

MUSICAL EXAMPLES AND CAPTIONS

Allow a quarter-inch between the top of a musical example and the text it follows, between the bottom of the example's caption and the text it precedes, and between the example itself and its caption. Place the caption beneath the example.

Production of Examples

For most classroom assignments, photocopied score examples, either collected at the end of a paper or pasted individually in between paragraphs of text, will be sufficient. (Your instructor may have different requirements, of course.) For graduate documents or works submitted for publication, it is far better to generate the examples you need with music-processing software such as FINALE or SCORE, or to pay someone to generate them. Such software enables authors to customize excerpts without having to include extra measures and to produce reductions that will be easier to read than full scores. (For works intended for publication, the musical examples need to be on separate sheets, not incorporated in the text.)

Works intended for publication and graduate documents to be bound and archived will often require permissions for the use of copyrighted musical material. The legalities regarding fair use (that is, scholarly, nonprofit use) of copyrighted material are complex, and it is necessary for authors to research each individual case, establishing who holds the rights and then formally asking permission. Obtaining permission will usually involve crediting the copyright holder in some way, usually on the page the example appears, and often it will require a fee. Music over 75 years old is generally within the public domain (meaning no longer under copyright), but a particular published *image* of it may not be (again, music-processing software will help in this situation). The rights to more recent music are often held by the publisher, and so—regardless of whether the examples are computer-generated or not—permissions must be obtained.

There are times, however, when it is better to leave examples out. When only passing reference is made to a musical passage, in a parenthetical context ("instances of the same phenomenon are found at the opening of Liszt's *Sonata in B Minor* and in measures 4-5 of Stephen Foster's 'Camptown Races,' but these were written much later than the Paradis example under discussion"), the reader can often do without the musical examples; the passages in question can be located for verification, if need be. A score example may also be avoided for reasons of familiarity; most readers will not need to review, say, the opening four notes of Beethoven's Fifth Symphony. Nor is it likely that many readers will need to see familiar popular songs (such as those by the Beatles) in notated form. (An exceptional case might be the discussion of a fine point in a Beatles song, such as the piano solo in "Rocky Raccoon.") But economy and restraint are as relevant to score examples as they are to words, and authors need to weigh the inclusion of each musical excerpt.

Captions

Every score example requires an individual caption, designated "Ex." for "example" (not "Fig." for "figure," which designates a chart or graph). Examples need to be numbered individually (i.e., Ex. 1, Ex. 2, etc.), and they may be put in subgroups (Ex. 1a, Ex. 1b, etc.) when the context demands it. For instance, a cluster of short, musically related examples, or different snippets of the same section of a piece, might constitute such a subgroup. In multi-chapter works such as theses, dissertations, and books, examples are sometimes numbered sequentially throughout the work, but it is preferable to number them according to chapter: those of chapter one will be numbered Ex. 1.1, 1.2, and 1.3; those of chapter two Ex. 2.1, 2.2, and so on.

Captions need to be complete, and they need to be uniform throughout a paper. Two basic schools of thought govern the contents of captions. One holds that each caption ought to have only the minimum necessary material: composer, piece, movement if necessary, and measure numbers of the passage provided. (For large scores with rehearsal numbers or letters but no numbered measures, it is common to use an indication such as "R2+3"—designating three measures after the measure marked with rehearsal number 2.) The following caption is typical of this school.

Ex. 38. Chopin, Nocturne op. 9/2, mm. 21-24.

This approach assumes that the only function of the caption is to identify the score example, and that any additional information belongs in the text and footnotes. Among the advantages of this philosophy is the ease of formatting; such captions do not often exceed one line, so typesetting and layout are relatively uncomplicated.

The other school of thought regards each musical example as operating both in relation to the main text and independently of it. A caption might therefore give (in addition to the identification provided in the first variety) far more information about the musical excerpt shown, such as its publisher, what the reader should be looking for in the excerpt, and other particulars. Such a caption might read:

> Ex. 38. Chopin, Nocturne op. 9/2, mm. 21-24 (Karol Mikuli edition), showing authentic variants stemming from the composer's own performance tradition. These variants were not included in Mikuli's 1880 edition of Chopin's works for Kistner in Leipzig, but rather in a separate edition of this single work by the same editor and publisher, "with the composer's authentic ornamentation."

The benefits to this approach include:

- all the material pertinent to the excerpted score itself is presented in close proximity to it
- the continuity of the text is not cluttered with tangential material
- certain kinds of information are thereby much easier for the reader to go back and find if needed

On the minus side:

- typesetting and formatting are much more problematic
- there is the possibility of the discussion becoming fragmented, with key elements remaining in the caption rather than in the text proper

Ultimately, this is a matter of taste, to be decided by the individual author, course instructor, or publisher, depending on the situation.

CITATIONS

Citations have two primary functions. First, they tell the reader—should the reader want to know, and reading the citations ought always to be the reader's option—where to find information that the author drew upon. Such information, whether in the form of direct quotations or paraphrases, must be cited properly, and these citations will then give appropriate credit for thoughts not the author's own. Second, proper citations allow readers to access the same sources the author did, to follow the author's train of thought, to proceed in different directions from these sources, and ultimately to evaluate the author's use and understanding of them. More information about when and how to cite sources is to be found in Chapter 6.

Citation formats vary somewhat throughout the English-speaking world. For the United States, the most concise and convenient source is D. Kern Holoman, *Writing About Music* (Berkeley and Los Angeles: University of California Press, 1988).[1] This work, a style manual for a prominent musicological journal, also provides guidance on a wide variety of other matters such as terminology, capitalization schemes, syllabification, and musical example formats. For further advice, particularly regarding academic documents and details of citation form, you will want to consult Kate L. Turabian, *A Manual for Writers of Term Papers, Theses, and Dissertations*, 6th ed. (Chicago and London: University of Chicago Press, 1996), which is a user-friendly summary of the *Chicago Manual of Style*. Note, however, that Turabian's *Manual* offers advice for a variety of fields and formats, so it must be used carefully, with the specific requirements of your situation in mind.

Turabian provides, for example, instructions for the system that uses parenthetical author-date citations, which is used by certain musical disciplines such as music education and ethnomusicology.

Liszt's reasons for writing in the Hungarian-Gypsy vein were in some measure personal as well as musical (Bellman 1993, 196).

This citation system depends upon the bibliography, to which the reader then turns. The date identifies which work by this author is meant when more than one work by the same author is listed. In the case of multiple works in the same year, "1993a," "1993b," and so on, solve the problem. The parenthetical author-date system unquestionably makes the citation process easier on the author, and it is probably for this reason that certain disciplines use it. It has, however, certain disadvantages:

---

[1] I differ with Holoman on a couple of points that bear acknowledgement. First, he advocates leaving the name of the publisher out of footnote citations; I agree with the many who include it. Second, he indicates page numbers with p. or pp.; I think these indications, in context, are unnecessary, and that the numbers themselves at the ends of footnotes are self-explanatory. You will find that there are minute differences among *all* style guides and that there is really no such thing as standard form.

- The parentheses needlessly chop up sentences and paragraphs, making the writing unattractive and the reading more laborious.
- This system forces the reader to read some citation material even when the reader may prefer not to, and there is no possibility that the citation material will appear on the same page as the parenthetical interruption.
- It requires a separate bibliography, which the standard footnote or endnote system does not.
- It *still* requires footnotes or endnotes when ancillary material other than a citation is needed.

In this matter, the requirements of the professor or the publisher take priority.

Finally, it is likely that you will encounter and use a bibliographic source that does not quite fit any given format. In such cases, try to follow principles gleaned from the examples given below and in Holoman and Turabian, make logical decisions, present all necessary information as clearly and succinctly as possible, and (in the words of my own dissertation advisor) "try to create something as beautiful as possible."

Three reminders:

- Number all footnotes. Footnote symbols such as asterisks are no longer used.
- Footnote citations always list the author's first name first. Bibliography entries always give the last name first because bibliographies are arranged alphabetically by author.
- Do not number bibliography entries; simply alphabetize them. Large bibliographies may be broken down into categories such as books, journal articles, and encyclopedia entries.

SAMPLE CITATIONS

For all the following examples, citations will be given in two forms: footnote (or endnote; format does not differ between them) and bibliography. The only difference between the two in terms of content is that bibliography citations, relating as they do to entire sources and not specific items of information, do not include individual page citations. (Since there is no doubt what the number or numbers at the end of a footnote mean, I and many others advocate omitting the use of "p." and "pp." for page and pages.) Footnote citations are indicated by a superscript number that appears at the end of the sentence or phrase that contains the information cited.

Books by One Author

Footnote

> [1]Robert Philip, *Early Recordings and Musical Style* (Cambridge: Cambridge University Press, 1992), 35-37.

Bibliography

> Philip, Robert. *Early Recordings and Musical Style*. Cambridge: Cambridge University Press, 1992.

Books by More Than One Author but Less Than Four

Footnote

> [2]Homer Ulrich and Paul A. Pisk, *A History of Music and Musical Style* (New York: Harcourt, Brace, 1963), 109.

Bibliography

> Ulrich, Homer, and Paul A. Pisk. *A History of Music and Musical Style*. New York: Harcourt, Brace, 1963.

Books by Four or More Authors

Footnote

> [3]Ahmed Suleiman and others, *Mid-American Musical Exoticism* (Cairo, IL: Exotica Publishers, 1922), 66.

Bibliography

> Suleiman, Ahmed, Mahmoud Nasar, Enrique Seixas, and Per Norquist. *Mid-American Musical Exoticism*. Cairo, IL: Exotica Publishers, 1922.

Books Translated or Edited

Footnote

> [4]Klára Hamburger, *Liszt*, trans. Gyula Gyulás (Budapest: Corvina Press, 1980), 35.

Bibliography

> Hamburger, Klára. *Liszt.* Translated by Gyula Gyulás. Budapest: Corvina Press, 1980.

Reprints of Earlier Works

Footnote

> [5]James Huneker, *Frédéric Chopin as Man and Musician* [1898] (New York: Dover, 1966), 42.

Bibliography

> Huneker, James. *Frédéric Chopin as Man and Musician* [1898]. New York: Dover, 1966.

Book with More Than One Edition, or for Which the Translation Is More Recent, or with More Than One Editor or Translator

Footnote

> [6]Jean-Jacques Eigeldinger, *Chopin: Pianist and Teacher* [1970], ed. Roy Howat, trans. Naomi Shohet with Krysia Osostowicz and Roy Howat (Cambridge: Cambridge University Press, 1986), 100-102.

Bibliography

> Eigeldinger, Jean-Jacques. *Chopin: Pianist and Teacher* [1970]. Edited by Roy Howat. Translated by Naomi Shohet with Krysia Osostowicz and Roy Howat. Cambridge: Cambridge University Press, 1986.

Note: The date of the original French edition is given in brackets so that the general age of the work, as opposed to that of the edition, may be ascertained.

Books with Additional Relevant Information Regarding Edition, etc.

Footnote

> [7]Joseph Machlis and Kristine Forney, *The Enjoyment of Music* [1955], 7th ed., Chronological Version (New York: W. W. Norton, 1995), 45.

Bibliography

> Machlis, Joseph, and Kristine Forney. *The Enjoyment of Music* [1955], 7th edition, Chronological Version. New York: W. W. Norton, 1995.

Article in an Encyclopedia or Dictionary, Unsigned

Footnote

> [8]*The New Harvard Dictionary of Music,* s.v. "Nationalism."

Note: Page numbers are unnecessary here; "s.v." stands for *sub verbo,* "under the word." (In music, well-known reference works are not generally listed in bibliographies, whether or not they have been cited in the footnotes.)

Article in an Encyclopedia or Dictionary, Signed

Footnote

> [9]Richard Orton, "Theremin," *The New Grove Dictionary of Music and Musicians,* ed. Stanley Sadie (London: Macmillan, 1980), vol. 18, 762.

Bibliography

> Orton, Richard. "Theremin." *The New Grove Dictionary of Music and Musicians,* ed. Stanley Sadie. London: Macmillan, 1980. Vol. 18, 762-63.

Note: Whether or not a *New Grove* article is cited in a bibliography depends on the scope of the article; something like Ian Bent's "Analysis" might well be. In classroom situations, your professor may want you to cite every source consulted.

Article or Chapter in an Anthology

Footnote

> [10]Jeffrey Kallberg, "Hearing Poland: Chopin and Nationalism," in *Nineteenth-Century Piano Music,* ed. R. Larry Todd (New York: Schirmer, 1990), 252-53.

Bibliography

> Kallberg, Jeffrey. "Hearing Poland: Chopin and Nationalism." In *Nineteenth-Century Piano Music,* 221-57. Edited by R. Larry Todd. New York: Schirmer, 1990.

Note: When referring to an article in a larger work, the footnote identifies the page numbers of the specific information cited, while the bibliography gives the page numbers of the entire article. This format differs slightly from that given in Turabian (6th ed., 11.26), so as to be consistent with the format of translated works.

Article in a Scholarly Journal

Footnote

> [11]Alejandro Enrique Planchart, "The Early Career of Guillaume Du Fay," *Journal of the American Musicological Society* XLVI/3 (Fall 1993), 348.

Bibliography

> Planchart, Alejandro Enrique. "The Early Career of Guillaume Du Fay." *Journal of the American Musicological Society* XLVI/3 (Fall 1993), 341-368.

Note: Some journals use Roman numerals to designate volume number, and some Arabic numerals; it is best to follow the journal's preference in this regard. Note that "XLVI/3," as opposed to "Vol. XLVI, no. 3," saves a good deal of space and presents the same information. Both comma (shown here) and colon are in common use, and therefore acceptable, to separate the journal volume and number (and parenthetical date) from the page reference.

Article in a Magazine

Footnote

> [12]Deborah Kauffman, "The Ideas (and Words) of Friedrich Wieck," *Piano and Keyboard,* January/February 1996, 39.

Bibliography

> Kauffman, Deborah. "The Ideas (and Words) of Friedrich Wieck." *Piano and Keyboard,* January/February 1996, 36-39.

Article in a Newspaper

Footnote

> [13]Ninotchka Bennahum, "Musical Modernismo," *The Village Voice,* 1 April 1997, 83.

Bibliography

> Bennahum, Ninotchka. "Musical Modernismo." *The Village Voice,* 1 April 1997, 83.

Note: Well-known newspapers, or those that include their place of origin in their names (e.g., the *Village Voice,* the *Los Angeles Times*), need not be identified geographically. In other cases, use parentheses for clarification: the *Progress-Bulletin* (Pomona, CA). When an article or news item is unsigned, simply begin the note with the title of the article or the headline appearing above it. In giving dates, "1 April 1998" is preferable to "April 1, 1998" because it does away with the comma. Newspaper articles are not usually listed in bibliographies.

Article or Foreword to an Edition of Music, Not by Composer

Footnote

> [14]Franz Liszt, "On John Field's Nocturnes" [1889], preface to John Field, *Eighteen Nocturnes* (New York: Schirmer, 1902), v.

Bibliography

> Liszt, Franz. "On John Field's Nocturnes." [1889] Preface to John Field, *Eighteen Nocturnes.* New York: Schirmer, 1902, iv-vi.

Note: The dates provided are those of the essay or preface and of the publication. Because publication histories of musical works tend to be very convoluted, it would be impossible to provide the same kind of information that one seeks to provide when citing other kinds of writing.

Moreover, since Field composed his nocturnes between 1812 and the mid-1830s, no single date would be sufficient to indicate when the pieces themselves originated.

The pagination is important here; the musical scores begin on page 1, but no pagination was provided for the front matter (title page, introductory essays, and so on). Such front matter is traditionally designated with lower-case roman numerals. When such pagination is provided, follow it; when it is not, start with the first page on which printing appears, be it the title page or something before, and count up from there (i.e., i, ii, iii, iv, etc.).

Article in or Preface to an Edition of Music, by Composer

Footnote

> [15]Colin McPhee, "Note," preface to the score of *Tabuh-Tabuhan* (New York: Associated Music Publishers, 1960), 3.

Bibliography

> McPhee, Colin. "Note." Preface to the score of *Tabuh-Tabuhan*. New York: Associated Music Publishers, 1960.

Note: Where there is no title, "Preface to the score of . . ." (without the quotation marks) is sufficient.

Liner or Jacket Notes to a Sound Recording

Footnote

> [16]Paul Williams, notes to Procol Harum, *Shine On Brightly* (1968), LP, A & M Records SP4151.

Bibliography

> Williams, Paul. Notes to Procol Harum, *Shine On Brightly*. LP, A & M Records SP4151, 1968.

Note: It is helpful to specify the kind of recording, e.g., Long-playing record (LP), Compact Disc (CD), Laserdisc (LD), Cassette, etc., when identifying the source. If there is a title to the essay, it should appear in quotation marks immediately after the author, but the words "notes to the recording" should still be used. (Since "liner notes," "jacket notes," "CD notes," "CD booklet," and so on, take up more space, the single word "notes" is sufficient.)

Listserv

Footnote

[17]Guido Adler, E-Mail to AMS-L (ams-l@virginia.edu; the American Musicological Society listserv), 1 April 1998.

Note: Given that electronic communication, by its very nature, encourages the instantaneous response and discourages reflection and verification, E-mail messages—particularly reactions or statements of opinion—cannot be considered as dependable as other kinds of sources. Nonetheless, in specific cases (a scholar's verification of a particular fact, for example) such communication may be used and cited. It may not be cited anonymously, regardless of whether the posting is public (i.e., to a listserv, bulletin board, or chat room) or private. (Internet posts are not cited in bibliographies.)

Personal E-Mail Correspondence

Footnote

[18]Eusebius Mandyczewski, personal E-mail, 1 April 1998.

Bibliography

(Internet posts are not cited in bibliographies.)

Website

Footnote

[19]Jonathan Berger, "Brahms at the Piano," http://www-ccrma.stanford.edu/~brg/brahms2.html (1998), accessed 24 April 1998.

Bibliography

Berger, Jonathan. "Brahms at the Piano." http://www-ccrma.stanford.edu/~brg/brahms2.html. 1998; accessed 24 April 1998.

Note: Try to keep website URLs ("URL" stands for Uniform Resource Locator, the long series of characters that constitutes the address of a specific website) on the same line, even if an inordinate number of spaces on a previous line results. Actual geographic location of the web author or the server on which the website is maintained is irrelevant; it is only necessary to provide the information that will enable the reader to find the same data you used.

Dates for both the material cited and the day you accessed the site are necessary because people update their websites and the information thereon can change or disappear. Because two dates can be confusing, it is important to distinguish between them by having the date of the website directly follow the URL, and by explicitly using the word "accessed" for the date you visited the site. When the author provides dates for creation and revision, include both: "March 1995, rev. December 1996," enclosed within the parentheses in the footnote form and placed before the semicolon in the bibliographic form.

FTP Sites and Gopher Sites are designed for the availability of text material only, as opposed to text and graphics (as is the case with websites). FTP Sites make documents available for ready downloading; Gopher Sites, now fast disappearing, were the precursors of modern websites that enabled users to navigate through menus of choices, to follow links, and so on. Citation form should follow that of websites because they are all sites that may be visited electronically and from which material may be downloaded. The URL will define what kind of site it is.

Explanatory Footnotes

It is common for footnotes to contain more than citations; they might evaluate a source or two or engage in a bit of parenthetical commentary that is relevant to the paper but would disturb the flow of the main text. In such cases, clarity and conciseness of wording is doubly necessary.

Footnote

[20]Here I follow Leonard Ratner's terminology, which defines a topic as a "subject of a musical discourse." Topics were composed of musical figures or surface characteristics that were identified with a common and well-understood dance type or musical style (see his *Classic Music: Expression, Form, and Style* [New York: Schirmer, 1980], 9-30).

Musical Scores

There is no general agreement on the citation of musical scores. When making a specific point about a score excerpt, you should provide a musical example, either photocopied or generated on music-processing software, complete with caption, as outlined in the previous section. Scores are almost never cited in footnotes; an in-text reference accompanied by the score example is sufficient.

Whether or not to include scores in bibliographies is a decision to be made by your professor or publisher. Musical scores are not often included in published bibliographies, but many professors want citations of all the resources a student author has used. Source studies, in which a variety of different editions (and, perhaps, manuscripts and sketches) are compared, require bibliographic citation of scores. The following formats may be used:

Bibliography

> Chopin, Frédéric. *Balladen.* Ed. Ewald Zimmerman. Munich: G. Henle, 1976.

> Chopin, Frédéric. *Trois eccosaises.* Manuscript score. 1826. Special Collections, Green Library, Stanford University, Stanford, CA.

> Holiday, David. *Four Dances for Twenty-Five Dollars.* 1985. Composer's Score.

Abbreviated Citation Form

When you refer to a source you have already cited, it is not necessary to give the full citation again. When the citations are consecutive, you need only use "Ibid.," short for Latin *ibidem* ("in the same place"), and the page numbers. When the citation is for the same page as in the previous citation, page numbers are unnecessary.

Footnote

[21]Ibid., 38. [Or just: [21]Ibid.]

Where the citations are not consecutive, give the author's last name, an abbreviated title of the book or article, and the page number. Here are abbreviated citations for citation examples 1 and 10, above:

Footnote

²²Philip, *Early Recordings*, 36.
²³Kallberg, "Hearing Poland," 255.

Note: The traditional forms "op. cit." (for books: "in the work [already] cited") and "loc. cit." (for articles: "in the place cited") are no longer used for abbreviated citations.

Last-Minute Corrections

Given even the very latest technology, you may find minor typographical errors in your submission draft, errors that you want to correct but for which you cannot justify using the paper for an additional printing. You may correct these typos in pen, delicately and neatly. Traditional manuscript editing symbols for such circumstances include:

beethoven the Composer	Capitalize; change to lower case
piano music	Insert a space
pinao	Reverse letters (or words)
piirano	Delete
pi ano	Close up space
¶	Begin a new paragraph here

Index